THE MAVERICK POETS

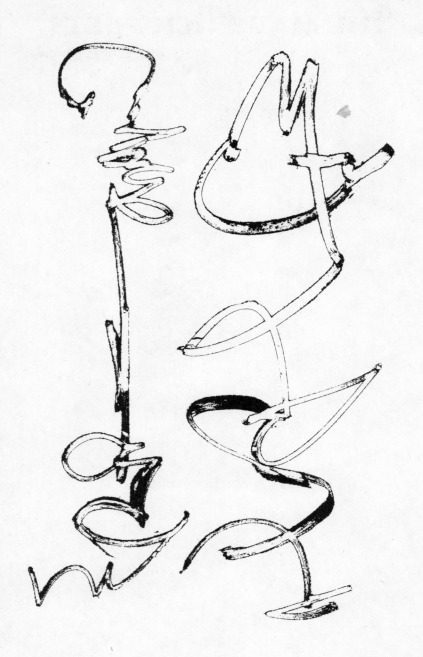

THE MAVERICK POETS

AN ANTHOLOGY

Edited by Steve Kowit

Gorilla Press
established 4004 B.C.

9269 Mission Gorge Road • Suite 229
Santee, CA 92071

THE MAVERICK POETS
an anthology
Edited by Steve Kowit

Cover art by Charles Bukowski
Typesetting by Mary L. Kowit — SoCal Graphics
Paste-up by Frank A. Baran

First Edition Second Printing 1989

Library of Congress Cataloging-in-Publication data

The Maverick Poets.

   1. American poetry--20th Century. I. Kowit, Steve.
PS 615.M39 1988   811'.54'08   88-81296

ISBN 0-9610454-2-6 (pbk.)
ISBN 0-9610454-3-4

Manufactured in the United States of America

Gorilla Press
9269 Mission Gorge Road • Suite 229
Santee, CA 92071

For Mary

CONTENTS

ART

AN INTRODUCTION

I will not have in my writing any elegance or effect or originality to hang in the way between me and the rest like curtains. I will have nothing hang in the way, not the richest curtains.
— Walt Whitman

In 1980, Alex Scandalios and I decided to edit an anthology of "easy" poetry for his *Willmore City Press*. "Easy" was Alex's word for a kind of straight-on, anti-rhetorical poetry written in the mother tongue: colloquial, hard edged and feisty — a brand of poetry that was easy to read but not, he liked to remind us, easy to write. Much of the work he had in mind had been inspired by Charles Bukowski, poet laureate of the disaffected, and was being published in off-beat literary magazines like *Nausea, Purr, Scree, Vagabond* and *The Wormwood Review*. It was an underground poetry that avoided the preciously self-conscious diction of mainstream verse on the one hand and the unrelenting incoherence of conventional avant-garde poetry on the other. It was gritty, raw, anecdotal, often funny, and seemed to us decidedly more interesting than the rather solemn stuff being touted by the respectable quarterlies. It was our contention that if the public had turned away from poetry it was due not to the pernicious influence of television or the incompetence of our schools or the technocratic bias of the culture, but simply to the fact that most of what was being published was ponderously obtuse and unrelievedly dull.

Alex and I worked on that "easy" poetry anthology for a year or so before abandoning it and going our separate ways: *Willmore City* folded, Alex got involved in other publishing ventures, and I went back to writing my poems. But I liked the idea too much to see it discarded altogether and vowed to bring out such a collection if the opportunity ever presented itself — or rather, I started thinking about putting together an anthology somewhat similar to the one we had planned but with significant differences. Although I wanted to include the best work being done in that L.A. hard-edged manner, there were other brands of accessible poetry that seemed just as exciting and fertile. For one, there was the "Beat" poetry that Allen Ginsberg and others had been fashioning since the fifties and which had opened up the possibilities of a contemporary Whitmanesque idiom — poems of a grander vision and bolder design than we had come to expect. It was at once an heroic and colloquial poetry: large-spirited, socially-engaged, heart-centered and defiantly wacky. If the Beat poets had never quite managed to rescue mainstream American verse from its gentility and hermetic aloofness, they had nevertheless proven that our poetry could be considerably more impassioned and convincing than the sort of verse being canonized by the academy.

But the territory I wanted to map included other poets too, poets who were not affiliated with either camp but who were equally committed to a poetry tuned to the spoken language, free of decorative rhetoric and distinguished by its clarity, humanity and power. My hope was to bring out a sizable anthology filled with the work of a large number of such writers, but in the end economic pressures forced me to pare the collection to its present size and many of those I had wanted to include simply had to be left out.

The poets in this collection have been called *mavericks* not to turn them into members of some new school but rather to emphasize that they share a common resistance to the pervasive style of late 20th century verse, with its debilitating preference for the tepid, mannered and opaque. But if the term also implies that the poets gathered here are spirited, outspoken, fiercely independent and happily disinclined to run with the herd — well, so much the better.

Steve Kowit
May, 1988

KIM ADDONIZIO

THE CALL

A man opens a magazine,
women with no clothes, their
eyes blacked out.
He dials a number,
hums a commercial
under his breath. A voice
tells him he can do
anything he wants to her.
He imagines standing her
against a wall, her saying
Oh baby you feel so good.
It's late. The woman
on the phone yawns,
trails the cord to the hall
to look in on her daughter.
She's curled with one
leg off the couch.
The woman shoulders the receiver,
tucks a sheet and whispers
Yes, do it, yes. She drifts
to the kitchen, opens
another Diet Pepsi, wonders how long
it will take him and where
she can find a cheap winter coat.
Remembering the bills, she flips off
the light. He's still saying *Soon,*
turning his wheelchair right,
left, right. A tube runs down
his pants leg. Sometimes
he feels something,
stops talking to concentrate
on movement down there.
Hello, the woman says.
You still on? She rubs a
hand over her eyes, blue
shadow comes off on her fingers.
Over the faint high hiss
of the open line
she hears the wheels knock
from table to wall.
What's that, she says.
Nothing, he tells her, and they both
listen to it.

BREAK

Through the open gate
the lambs escape.
They stand in the road.
The farmer's off
scything the wheat.
Bawling, or staring
stupidly, they're not sure
why they're out here
in the gravel and dust.
Deep down they sense
their fate: the slow thaw
into the dish drainer,
the knife sawing towards
the bone, the long dissolve
with gin and asparagus.
Their cropped tails twitch.
A truck swerves by.
MATT'S MEATS. They mill
and bleat, crowding
onto the shoulder. Matt
pulls over, runs at them
waving his fat arms
and screaming *G'yup! Shoo!*
The spooked lambs
stampede for the gate
and squeeze through.
They line up at the fence
to watch Matt as he passes.
Suddenly they're tired,
and starving
for some grain with molasses.

ALTA

all those men puppy dogging
round my door. it was like
playing "go in & out the window"
& they were all jealous sillies,
as if any of them had ever known me.
the woman they possessed so hard didnt even exist.
& i can't remember their names to call them
& laugh over the phone.

that chick is SO REVOLUTIONARY
she dresses poor on purpose.
she eschews the boozhwa comforts like
washing machines, male lovers, &
flush toilets. i mean she is
EVERY KIND of revolutionary!
she'd bum off her friends before she'd work
in a counter-revolutionary government job!
(how come she can afford to be so revolutionary?)
i mean, this chick is SO REVOLUTIONARY,
she laughs at housewives, agrees that
we're an inferior breed.
she would never have a kid if she could have
an abortion instead. get it? this chick is
SELF FULFILLED!
super chick   ta daa!
even her period glows in the dark.

L.O.L.
little old ladies is the term they use
to make us laugh at the women who
have been fighting for 60 years.

the old wicker chair unravelling.
& him snoring, asleep on my right.
& too early we have to wake & get the children
& bring them home & any day now
i'll be happy.
i mean really. really happy.

SHIRLEY 4 YEARS LATER

i was all self-righteous
when you came to visit
my overcleaned 3 bedroom home
in san lorenzo. yr baby
had diaper rash; i was superior;
my kid never even had a leaky nose.
your hair looked like mine does now.
you wore a white shirt, jeans, boots;
yr cigarette flapped on yr lip
as you talked, i sat primly shocked
& wondered why i ever (flash/ yr head in my lap
your delicate scarred fingertips on the back of
my neck, you pull me down & raise yr open mouth/
grass growing, trees, the brickbarred asylum, our kiss,
our kiss) why i ever hungered
for you, my legs crossed in my beige
carpeted living room.

the girls with their young breasts
black hair hiding their necks
they are laughing at the boys
"ai muchachos!" & i hide
my feelings for them, i
look out the window of the bus
at shops with broken windows

ah. yr angry.
amazing how people hop to my side if i just lie down naked.
amazing how they attack me if i dont.
at least you dont claim to love me.
i'm always grateful for small favours.

joy comes so softly sometimes i dont hear it.
i'm too busy bitching & flailing my arms.
but it sneaks in anyway: the baby blowing kisses
or grass splitting apart pavement.

ANTLER

REXROTH AS HE APPEARED TO EXIST
MARCH 24, 1968 9:00 PM

It was as if he were slowly falling asleep,
Sitting in that chair, while everyone at the party
    asked him questions.
Suddenly I wondered if someday I'd become a bard
And if, as they asked me questions,
    I'd tilt back my head and for a minute or two
    pretend to doze, eyes peering under lids,
And I wondered if then, in that future crowd,
There'd be anyone like me who once
    couldn't think of any questions to ask,
And couldn't help but think: how soon
    he will be dead
And that's how he'll look in the coffin,
    head back like that
    with Halley's Comet hair.
Years from now when I hear the news of his death
I'll remember that night and this poem,
Shivering a little as I did then,
Surprising myself
    with the thought of salmon
    shooting up the rapids of his brain,
What he was — near as a grosbeak, far as Orion,
    the sound of mice moving delicately
    in the walls of his flesh.

"YOUR POETRY'S NO GOOD BECAUSE
IT TRIES TO CONVEY A MESSAGE"

Tell it to Jews hanging from meathooks,
Tell it to Wilfred Owen's exploded face,
Tell it to James Wright's cancerous cut-out tongue,
Tell it to Victor Jara's hands chopped off
    in Santiago Stadium,
Tell it to all the ears, breasts, cocks and balls
    cut off in every war,
Tell it to all the beautiful eyes
    gouged out in every war,
Tell it to the pyramid of human skulls
    that never stops growing,
Tell it to the decapitated head held up
    to gape twitching corpse jeering crowd,
Tell it to the fact we're all in Auschwitz because
    any second every city can become Holocaust,
Tell it to Hetch Hetchy, tell it to Glen Canyon,
    tell it to Wounded Knee and the Buffalo,

Tell it to the aluminum fibers in your brain
            and the cancer in your food and water
            which will eventually kill you,
Tell it to 100 trillion cigarettes a year,
Tell it to 100 billion spent on war every minute,
Tell it to Johnny Got His Gun,
Tell it to the ashes of Neruda's library,
Tell it to 52 million children under 15
            working in factories in Southeast Asia,
Tell it to more people born in 2984
            than all the people ever born,
Tell it to the annihilated White Pine dominions
            of Wisconsin,
Tell it to the Sequoias still standing
            who were alive one thousand years
            before the Bible was written,
Tell it to all the unexperienced homosexual joy
            since Christianity came into power,
Tell it to the $100,000 it cost to kill
            each soldier in World War II,
Tell it to Henry Ford's factory in France
            that made tanks for the Third Reich,
Tell it to the sunrise, tell it to the rainbow,
            tell it to the flower made love to by the bee,
Tell it to the waterfall that never stops telling,
Tell it to the combers that never cease crashing,
Tell it to the reflection of stars
            in the rain-filled blackbear track,
Tell it to the canyons that echo
            the canyons that echo,
Tell it to the birdsong, whalesong, wolfsong, cricketsong,
Tell it to the clouds as they float overhead,
            yell it to the lightning, bell it to the thunder,
            well it to the pouring rain, spell it
            on kindergarten blackboard,
            knell it to firefly cemetery dusk,
Tell it to tombstones who have forgotten their names,
Tell it to the shadow of your breathcloud
            on a winter day,
Tell it to mother harp seals
            while their babies are skinned alive,
Tell it to the naked black youth being hung
            by white lynchmob while they point and laugh,
Tell it to the geniuses who invent better and better
            methods of mass murder,
Tell it to the stockpiles of suicide pills
            to be dispensed in the event of apocalypse,
Tell it to the fact more women raped in America every year
            than poetry books sold every year,
Tell it to the statistics of ecocide, genocide, suicide,
Tell it to Kennedy's brainfragments
            quivering on the Dallas street,
Tell it to Sylvia Plath's head in the oven,
Tell it to Lorca while the soldier fires
            two bullets up his ass,
Tell it to Ishi on the L.A. Freeway during rush hour,
Tell it to Black Elk on Times Square at midnight
            on New Year's Eve,
Tell it to the Blue Whales and Redwoods
            murdered by harpoons and buzz-saws,
Tell it to the shadowgraphs in Hiroshima,
Tell it to the poets on Skid Row.

FACTORY
(from Part X)

Is it necessary to list
      every machine necessary to extract raw materials
      every machine necessary to transport them
      and every machine necessary to transform them
           into iron, steel, aluminum
      and everything made from iron, steel, aluminum,
      and every machine necessary to make it?
What do I get for unveiling the machinery that makes
      footballs, baseballs, basketballs, tennisballs,
      bowlingballs, billiardballs, pingpongballs, snowmobiles,
      boxinggloves, golfclubs, sailboats, surfboards,
      scubagear, bathtubs, and easychairs?
Must we see the slaves behind *every* device of recreation and leisure?
Must we see the slaves behind *every* laborsaving device?
(Do you think it's trite to call them slaves?
Are you only a company man for Literature
      slaving on the disassembly line of criticism?
Are you only a cog in the Poetry Factory?
How many poems by Zinjanthropus
      appear in your Immortal Anthology?)
Wheelbarrow factories! Kitchen sink capitalisms!
Staplegun generalissimos! Toothpick presidents!
Paper czars! Linoleum pharaohs!
Punchpress emperors! Pushbutton potentates!
Monopoly millionaires! Deodorant billionaires!
Electricity trillionaires! Computer quadrillionaires!
Quintillionaires of wood! Sextillionaires of rock!
Septillionaires of plastic! Octillionaires of oil!
Nonillionaires of flesh! Decillionaires of Oblivion!
      The exact number of pennies ever made!
      The exact number of papercups ever made!
      The exact number of number two pencils ever made!
More rope! More tape! More pipe! More fence!
More wallets! More purses! More needles! More thread!
More envelopes! More stamps! More brushes! More paint!
More boxes! More bottles! More screws! More screwdrivers!
More washingmachines! More airconditioners! More vacuum cleaners!
      More flashlight batteries!
Dynamos stretching to the horizon and still not enough!
More generators! More blastfurnaces! More concrete! More antennae!
Capitalisms of thumbtacks and thumbscrews!
Stockholders in tongue-depressors and rectal thermometers!
Manufacturers of lawnmowers, snowblowers, toenail clippers and
      machetes!
World's largest producers of arrows, slingshots, fishhooks,
      riflesights, decoys, traps, and raccoon death-cry calls!
Peddlers of pills and more pills and pill containers
      and prescription forms!
Industries for the Blind! Industries for the Retarded!
Where artificial flavor and color are made!
Where artificial flowers and grass are made!
Where artificial eyes and arms and legs are made!
      and wherever they make boobytraps!
      and wherever they make tiddlywinks!
      and wherever they make doors and doorknobs
          and doorbells and hinges and locks and keys!
Corporations of bulletproof vests and silencers!

Corporations of blowtorches, rivetguns and girders!
(And where do dildoes and bathyspheres fit in?)
Every breath more parkingmeters and bankvaults
        and armored trucks and turnstiles
        and wedding rings and vagina dolls
        and rubbers and rubberbands
        and rubber rafts and lifepreservers
        and thingamabobs and thingamadoodles
        and gargle and garbage trucks
                and garbage cans
                and sprinkling cans
                and aerosol cans
                and "Eat" signs
                and "Stop" signs
                and "No Trespassing" signs
        and switchboards and turbines
        and conveyor belts of conveyor belts!
And the world's largest producers of machineguns and chainsaws!
And 20,000 a day extermination factory of Auschwitz!
And one billion gallons of gasoline burned in California each month!
And 38 cigarettes inhaled every day in New York City
        just by breathing the air!
And even you, backpacks, compasses, and maps of the wild!
        must you be from factories!
Et tu mountain climbing gear?
And even icecream and kaleidoscopes
        and bubblewands and balloons
                and swingsets and teetertotters
                and yoyos and marbles
                and frisbees and skateboards
                and pinwheels and merrygorounds
                and beanies with propellers
                and the hall of mirrors?
Must we see the slaves behind every toy of our childhood?
Must we see the gypped lives behind the pantheon of laughs?
        O souls flophoused by factories!
        O geniuses imbeciled by factories
        O enlightenment shoplifted by factories!
Copying machine factories! Calculating machine factories!
Vending machine factories! Change machine factories!
Humans spending their lives making lipstick or eyeshadow!
Humans spending their lives making crystal balls or fortune cookies!
Humans spending their lives making calendars or blindman canes!
Working your way up to foreman in the insecticide factory!
Working your way up to employment manager in the squirtgun factory!
Working your way up to the top in the pay toilet factory!
        40 years making piggybanks!
        480 months making burglar alarms or handcuffs!
        2000 weeks making wind chimes, wind machines
                or wind-up toys!
        10,400 days of your life
                making stopwatches or metronomes!
        83,200 hours of your life
                making miniature replicas of Rodin's Thinker!
        4,992,000 minutes of your life
                gluing the hemispheres of globes together!
        299,952,000 seconds of your life
                cranking out the links of chains!

CHILDFOOT VISITATION

One night traveling a Green Tortoise bus
   San Francisco to Seattle,
The rear of the bus converted to pads for sleeping,
Sleeping on my back as we plunged through pouring rain,
   the other weary passengers sleeping,
Suddenly something moving in my beard and under my nose
   woke me up —
Opening my eyes in the darkness
   I saw in the flickering headlight patterns
   of passing cars
The small foot of the little girl sleeping
   beside her mother.
Cleansmelling childfoot flower stretching beneath my nose
   as she changed position in her dream.
Gently pushing it away, careful not to wake her,
   I drifted off to sleep
Thinking how many men who never had a child
   are visited by a childhood foot
   slowly sliding through their beards
   opening their eyes to
   its perfect shape in the twilight?
Suddenly out of Eternity coming to me
   white and pink and smelling good,
For the first time in my life
   a little girl's naked foot
   woke me up.

FRANK BIDART

ANOTHER LIFE

> *Peut-être n'es-tu pas suffisamment mort.*
> *C'est ici la limite de notre domaine. Devant*
> *toi coule un fleuve.*
>
> *Valéry*

"—In a dream I never *exactly* dreamed,
but that is, somehow, the quintessence
of what I *might* have dreamed,

Kennedy is in Paris

again; it's '61; once again
some new national life seems possible,
though desperately, I try to remain unduped,
even cynical . . .

He's standing in an open car,

brilliantly lit, bright orange
next to a grey de Gaulle, and they stand
not far from me, slowly moving up the Champs-Elysées . . .

Bareheaded in the rain, he gives a short
choppy wave, smiling like a sun god.

—I stand and
look, suddenly at peace; once again mindlessly
moved,

as they bear up the fields of Elysium

the possibility of Atlantic peace,

reconciliation between all that power, energy,
optimism,—

and an older wisdom, without
illusions, without force, the austere source
of nihilism, corrupted only by its dream of Glory . . .

But no—; as I
watch, the style is

not quite right—;

Kennedy is *too* orange . . .

And de Gaulle, white, dead
white, ghost white, not even grey . . .

As my heart
began to grieve for my own awkwardness and
ignorance, which would never be
soothed by the informing energies

of whatever

wisdom saves,—

I saw a young man, almost

my twin, who had written
                    'MONSTER'
in awkward lettering with a crayon across
the front of his sweat shirt.
                              He was gnawing on his arm,

in rage and anger gouging up
pieces of flesh—; but as I moved to stop him, somehow
help him,
          suddenly he looked up,

and began, as I had, to look at Kennedy and de Gaulle:

and then abruptly, almost as if I were seeing him
through a camera lens, his figure

split in two,—
              or doubled,—

and all the fury
                 drained from his stunned, exhausted face . . .

But only for a moment. Soon his eyes turned down
to the word on his chest. The two figures
again became one,

and with fresh energy he attacked the mutilated arm . . .

—Fascinated, I watched as this
pattern, this cycle,
                    repeated several times.

Then he reached out and touched me.

—Repelled,
           I pulled back . . . But he became
frantic, demanding that I become
the body he split into:
                        'It's harder
to manage *each* time! Please,
give me your energy;—*help me!*'
                                 I said it was impossible,
there was *no part* of us the same:
we were just watching a parade together:
(and then, as he reached for my face)
                                      leave me *alone!*

He smirked, and said
I was never alone.
                   I told him to go to hell.

He said that this was hell.

                    —I said it was impossible,
there was *no part* of us the same:
we were just watching a parade together:
                                        when I saw

Grief, avenging Care, pale
Disease, Insanity, Age, and Fear,
                                 —all the raging desolations

which I had come to learn were my patrimony;
the true progeny of my parents' marriage;
the gifts hidden within the mirror;

—standing guard at the gate of this place,
triumphant,

striking poses
               eloquent of the disasters they embodied . . .
—I took several steps to the right, and saw
Kennedy was paper-thin,
             as was de Gaulle;
mere cardboard figures
whose possible real existence
lay buried beneath a million tumbling newspaper photographs . . .

—I turned, and turned, but now all that was left
was an enormous
         fresco;—on each side, the unreadable
              fresco of my life . . ."

LAUREL ANN BOGEN

I COULDA BEEN A CONTENDER

I got it back
pug-scrappy
I almost tossed out
the frenzy and the cockroaches
for a split-level mirage
of dubious companionship

I've been workin' out
I got back
my high school year book
I so diligently lent you
because you said you wanted
to see what I looked like
before my nose job
I got back my Gordon Lightfoot
albums I couldn't play
because they weren't hip enough
I got back
my dancer's legs
and my depressing poems

I was mainlining insecurity
I was giving up my shot
at the Middleweight Championship of the world
for cheese enchiladas and midnight assignations
I didn't know
that I came so cheap

Meeting you taught me
the meaning of free enterprise
I don't have to barter
for love
I can go the distance
I have got the off-key song
and the lop-sided smile
and the Ali shuffle
and no amount
of Maternal Understanding
is going to make you anything more
than a manipulator of affections
a sparring partner to my heart

I don't need it anymore
I have enough bullshit of my own
than to cope with yours

I got it all back —
the call,
the blue-white voltage,
the singular identity —
I have escaped
with my life

I EAT LUNCH WITH A SCHIZOPHRENIC

I check for gestapo agents
under the table
there are no electronic bugs
in the flowers
we talk freely
about jamming devices
and daredevil escapes
The waitress asks
if everything's OK
I tell her fine
except for the two SS officers
sitting drinking Rob Roys
pretending not to watch us
They slip a secret message
on the check —
Please pay when served —
Dollars or marks
I ask
She says just pay up
and spits out her gum
on the napkin
Her nametag says Barbi
I don't want to make a scene
so I pay the bill
and glance at my jr. hypnotist watch
Large segments of the world's population
have been converted by this time
saving machine
I strap to my wrist
disguised as a timex
I turn it on the SS officers
They think nothing's changed
but we know different
We know the allies
are going to bust
in here with tear gas
and submachine guns
looking for nazi jew-haters

The problem's not in the hamburgers
chili
or cokes
I explain
the problem is in being susceptible

LOVERNE BROWN

A SUNDAY MORNING AFTER
A SATURDAY NIGHT

She's so happy, this girl,
she's sending out sparks like a brush fire,
so lit with life
her eyes could beam airplanes through fog,
so warm with his loving
we could blacken our toast
on her forehead.

The phone rings
and she whispers to it
"I love you."
The cord uncoils
and leaps to tell him
she said it,
the receiver melts in her hand
as if done by Dali,
the whole room crackles

and we at the breakfast table
smile
but at safe distance
having learned by living
that love so without insulation
can immolate more than the toast.

CHECKMATE

That sense of peril
endemic to the times we live in,
keeping nerve and eye alert
as we hurtle down freeways,
that tells us the footsteps behind us
as we walk a dark street
are boding no good
and it's time to run for it,

leans on my shoulder now
in the voting booth
as I lift my hand
to opt for the politician
I think least likely
to light the fuse of our finish,
and it palsies the hand
with churlish mutterings
of the long sad list
of my previous miscalculations.

19

THE WARNING

An innocent evening
good talk and wine with a friend
wind rustles the curtains
a stereo plays

a moment when neither of us speaks

then suddenly the merest flutter
of warning

as if a snake's tail
flipped once as it disappeared
under the bookcase

as if my eye caught beneath the draperies
the feet of a strange someone
moving backward to escape my eye

something has changed in the room

ice forms at the nape of my neck
my flesh sinks inward upon my bones
I stare at my glass
see it falling slowly, slowly,
to bounce twice on the carpet
with a frivolous splash of claret
and no noise

it is only for a moment
I look up into unperturbed eyes
my glass has not really
fallen
my escape is not blocked
my coat is brought to me
our goodbyes are easy.

Why then do I stand
in the safety of my own room,
my back to a locked door
and my hand on a jackhammer heart,
my throat arched against a danger
all the more menacing
because the fingers are known?

SHELL GAMES

On the night of his sixtieth birthday
while taking his shoes off
Chandler arrived at a truth—
he was always a failure;
never able to pick the shell
the money was under,
or the house with a garden to dig in—
too trusting, too much a fool,
to guess that the shells were all empty.

Undressing silently, so as not to disturb
the woman who shared his room, a delicate woman
who had wed him expecting more,
tried hard to be happy with less,
he looked at his lean torso and told himself

he could still do anything, almost,
if people would let him;
he still remembered schematics of B-52s
whose bellies he crawled in during World War II:
proud of his job, then, sure of his burgeoning future,
in the flush of good fortune he married
and his namesake was born.

But the jobs never came after that,
never the good ones;
he went to Korea a soldier, came back unemployed,
started a business that failed,
worked for a firm that went under,
spent a decade or more at a table assembling computers,
for the past two years was a guard in a nuclear plant,
till a dry cough riddled his lungs
and his wife grew fearful,
claiming he sparked in the night,
like foxfire, she told him.

He sat on the edge of the mattress and lit a cigarette,
daring his lungs to resent it; they did,
and he hunched his back till the pain and the rattle was gone.
"So, the shells were all empty," he muttered—
"the hell with it all, then."

Somehow this absolved him; he slid into bed
and lay there smoking, staring at his country's flag,
which straddled the mildewed wall to keep the chill out.
The only thing his government ever gave him,
he saw it first draped soberly over the box
his son came home in, loser in still another
and deadlier shell game in Vietnam.
When they offered the flag, and he flinched,
not wanting to touch it:
"Take it," the chaplain said.
"Won't cost you nothing. It's free!"

A VERY WET LEAVETAKING

Comrades, I regret to inform you
I'm about to abandon this project.
The city cannot be saved,
does not deserve to be saved,
does not want to be saved—
since our warning cries went unanswered,
since, though the night was clear,
they chose to remain
with Merv and Johnny and carcinogenic beer.

Our own involvement was simple,
a matter of timing.
These holes appeared in this dike
and we were here.
We remembered that big-thumbed kid,
the hero of Holland,

and thought we could hold back the sea
till the townsmen came.

Well, the night's half over;
it's plain that they're not coming;
the tide is high and
the holes in the dike grow larger.
My arm is too small a cork
and floats in the flood,
and I must tell you
with shame but in all honesty
I am not yet fully committed
to sticking my head in.

MEETING OF MAVERICKS

Milkweed grows by my fence.
Don't ask me to pull it.
Weeds were my friends in childhood—
emerald explosions
in the dull cinders of train track,
green lace at the sleeves
of our water trough.
Eyes starved for color
were well fed by fireweed
elbowing tin cans aside
to take over the dump.

I live in the city now,
but claim kinship whenever
the uncombed head of a dandelion
pops up like a gopher
in the midst of a groomed lawn,
or a purple thistle—
remembered from roadside ditches—
looms insolent
in an enclave of roses.

Today a prickly thing
I don't know the name of
is exploiting a crack
in our sidewalk.
I greet it as friend:

"Hello, I too
like to challenge the fissures
in my firmament,
squeeze through, sometimes,
more often fracture my skull."

My new acquaintance braces his spine
along the crack, and shoves.
Cement crumbles.

I think tonight
I will sneak out and water
this one!

WILD GEESE

That last October, summer delayed her going,
held time enchanted, even while sun slipped southward,
kept birches green, blackberries on the vine,
one perfect rose to dazzle our bedroom window,
drove back the rain, allowed no cloud in her kingdom.

Then the wild geese curved over,
with a shrill of wings and deep-bell cries,
inscribing a magic triangle on the blank sky.
We could not read the sign— but summer fled,
birches slid into autumn, yellow as pumpkins,
reddening bushes dropped their dry berries dustward,
the perfect rose came perfectly apart,
tossing its petals into a spiraling wind.

One night the rain came, singing and jubilant,
and we curled into each other and slept, not knowing
the sign of the wild geese was upon us, too,
and this was our last October to be together.

ARRIVAL IN EARLY MORNING

Hello, my cool grey home,
my weathered sea-town—
pier gleaming abalone in the mist—
I'm back again, as I always meant to be;
our boat, a prancing pony, nuzzles the piling,
the wet rope ladder leans to accept our climb,
we walk catfooted through a feathery fog
over splintered boards
fish scales
salt   sand
past the piled nets
and the drooping nets of the dories
toward a blue shore
sending out signals of cedar.

The mist rises suddenly
like a panic of doves
white day slides down the mountain.
We see Sven Carlson's cabin
the door open
Sven running toward us laughing
with arms outstretched. . .

There will be many more welcomes
as we take the plank road into town
but I think I will use up all of my tears
on this one.

CHARLES BUKOWSKI

BEANS WITH GARLIC

this is important enough:
to get your feelings down,
it is better than shaving
or cooking beans with garlic.
it is the little we can do
this small bravery of knowledge
and there is of course
madness and terror too
in knowing
that some part of you
wound up like a clock
can never be wound again
once it stops.
but now
there's a ticking under your shirt
and you whirl the beans with a spoon,
one love dead, one love departed
another love . . .
ah! as many loves as beans
yes, count them now
sad, sad
your feelings boiling over flame,
get this down.

THE INSANE ALWAYS LOVED ME

and the subnormal.
all through grammar school
junior high
high school
junior college
the unwanted would attach
themselves to
me.
guys with one arm
guys with twitches
guys with speech defects
guys with white film
over one eye,

cowards
misanthropes
killers
peep-freaks
and thieves.
and all through the
factories and on the
bum
I always drew the
unwanted. they found me
right off and attached
themselves. they
still do.
in this neighborhood now
there's one who's
found me.
he pushes around a
shopping cart
filled with trash:
broken canes, shoelaces,
empty potato chip bags,
milk cartons, newspapers, penholders . . .
"hey, buddy, how ya doin' ?"
I stop and we talk a
while.
then I say goodbye
but he still follows
me
past the beer
parlours and the
love parlours . . .
"keep me *informed,*
buddy, keep me *informed,*
I want to know what's
going on."
he's my new one.
I've never seen him
talk to anybody
else.
the cart rattles
along a little bit
behind me
then something
falls out.
he stops to pick
it up.
as he does I
walk through the
front door of the
green hotel on the corner
pass down through
the hall
come out the back
door and
there's a cat
shitting there in
absolute delight,
he grins at me.

BUK

THE DRILL

our marriage book, it
says.
I look through it.
they lasted ten years.
they were young once.
now I sleep in her bed.
he phones her:
"I want my drill back.
have it ready.
I'll pick the children up at
ten."
when he arrives he waits outside
the door.
his children leave with
him.
she comes back to bed
and I stretch a leg out
place it against hers.
I was young once too.
human relationships simply aren't
durable.
I think back to the women in
my life.
they seem non-existent.

"did he get his drill?" I ask.

"yes, he got his drill."

I wonder if I'll ever have to come
back for my bermuda
shorts and my record album
by *The Academy of St. Martin in the
Fields*? I suppose I
will.

THE HISTORY OF A TOUGH MOTHERFUCKER

he came to the door one night wet thin beaten and
terrorized
a white cross-eyed tailless cat
I took him in and fed him and he stayed
grew to trust me until a friend drove up the driveway
and ran him over
I took what was left to a vet who said, "not much
chance . . . give him these pills . . . his backbone
is crushed, but it was crushed before and somehow
mended, if he lives he'll never walk, look at
these x-rays, he's been shot, look here, the pellets
are still there . . . also, he once had a tail, somebody
cut it off . . ."

I took the cat back, it was a hot summer, one of the
hottest in decades, I put him on the bathroom
floor, gave him water and pills, he wouldn't eat, he
wouldn't touch the water, I dipped my finger into it
and wet his mouth and I talked to him, I didn't go any-
where, I put in a lot of bathroom time and talked to
him and gently touched him and he looked back at
me with those pale blue crossed eyes and as the days went
by he made his first move
dragging himself forward by his front legs
(the rear ones wouldn't work)
he made it to the litter box
crawled over and in,
it was like the trumpet of possible victory
blowing in that bathroom and into the city, I
related to that cat — I'd had it bad, not that
bad but bad enough . . .

one morning he got up, stood up, fell back down and
just looked at me.

"you can make it," I said to him.

he kept trying, getting up and falling down, finally
he walked a few steps, he was like a drunk, the
rear legs just didn't want to do it and he fell again, rested,
then got up.

you know the rest: now he's better than ever, cross-eyed,
almost toothless, but the grace is back, and that look in
his eyes never left . . .

and now sometimes I'm interviewed, they want to hear about
life and literature and I get drunk and hold up my cross-eyed,
shot, runover de-tailed cat and I say, "look, look
at *this!*"

but they don't understand, they say something like, "you
say you've been influenced by Celine?"

"no," I hold the cat up, "by what happens, by
things like this, by this, by *this!*"

I shake the cat, hold him up in
the smoky and drunken light, he's relaxed he knows . . .

it's then that the interviews end
although I am proud sometimes when I see the pictures
later and there I am and there is the cat and we are photo-
graphed together.

he too knows it's bullshit but that somehow it all helps.

27

THE PROUD THIN DYING

I see old people on pensions in the
supermarkets and they are thin and they are
proud and they are dying
they are starving on their feet and saying
nothing. long ago, among other lies,
they were taught that silence was
bravery. now, having worked a lifetime,
inflation has trapped them. they look around
steal a grape
chew on it. finally they make a tiny
purchase, a day's worth
another lie they were taught:
thou shalt not steal.
they'd rather starve than steal
(one grape won't save them)
and in tiny rooms
while reading the market ads
they'll starve
they'll die without a sound
pulled out of roominghouses
by young blond boys with long hair
who'll slide them in
and pull away from the curb, these
boys
handsome of eye
thinking of Vegas and pussy and
victory.
it's the order of things: each one
gets a taste of honey
then the knife.

TAKE IT

got it down so tight the hinges squeaked.
threw out all three cats
drove over the two bridges
picked up $414.00 at the harness races
came in
listened to Shostakovich's First
then finally
cleaned the ring out of the bathtub
filled it
bathed while drinking a bottle of
chilled white wine
then
toweled off
got into bed
legs pointed east
I
inhaled
then
let it out:
the pain and defeat
of the world.
then I
slept like a baby
with big fat balls and
silver hair.

CLEAN OLD MAN

here I'll be
55 in a
week.

what will I
write about
when it no
longer stands
up in the morning?

my critics
will love it
when my playground
narrows down to
tortoises
and shellstars.

they might even
say
nice things about
me

as if I had
finally
come to my
senses.

RAYMOND CARVER

THE AUTHOR OF HER MISFORTUNE

For the world is the world,
And it writes no histories
that end in love.
— Stephen Spender

I'm not the man she claims. But
this much is true: the past is
distant, a receding coastline,
and we're all in the same boat,
a scrim of rain over the sea-lanes.
Still, I wish she wouldn't keep on
saying those things about me!
Over the long course
everything but hope lets you go, then
even that loosens its grip.
There isn't enough of anything
as long as we live. But at intervals
a sweetness appears and, given a chance,
prevails. It's true I'm happy now.
And it'd be nice if she
could hold her tongue. Stop
hating me for being happy.
Blaming me for her life. I'm afraid
I'm mixed up in her mind
with someone else. A young man
of no character, living on dreams,
who swore he'd love her forever.
One who gave her a ring, and a bracelet.
Who said, *Come with me. You can trust me.*
Things to that effect. I'm not that man.
She has me confused, as I said,
with someone else.

RAIN

Woke up this morning with
a terrific urge to lie in bed all day
and read. Fought against it for a minute.

Then looked out the window at the rain.
And gave over. Put myself entirely
in the keep of this rainy morning.

Would I live my life over again?
Make the same unforgiveable mistakes?
Yes, given half a chance. Yes.

THE HAT

Walking around on our first day
in Mexico City, we come to a sidewalk café
on Reforma Avenue where a man in a hat
sits drinking a beer.
At first the man seems just like any
other man, wearing a hat, drinking a beer
in the middle of the day. But next to this man,
asleep on the broad sidewalk, is a bear
with its head on its paws. The bear's
eyes are closed, but not all the way. As if
it were there, and not there. Everyone

is giving the bear a wide berth.
But a crowd is gathering too, bulging
out onto the Avenue. The man has
a chain around his waist. The chain
goes from his lap to the bear's collar,
a band of steel. On the table
in front of the man rests an iron bar
with a leather handle. And as if this
were not enough, the man drains the last
of his beer and picks up the bar.
Gets up from the table and hauls
on the chain. The bear stirs, opens its
mouth — old brown and yellow fangs.
But fangs. The man jerks on the chain,
hard. The bear rises to all fours now
and growls. The man slaps the bear on
its shoulder with the bar, bringing
a tiny cloud of dust. Growls something
himself. The bear waits while the man takes
another swing. Slowly, the bear rises
onto its hind legs, swings at air and at
that goddamned bar. Begins to shuffle
then, begins to snap its jaws as the man
slugs it again, and, yes, again

with that bar. There's a tambourine.
I nearly forgot that. The man shakes
it as he chants, as he strikes the bear
who weaves on its hind legs. Growls
and snaps and weaves in a poor dance.
This scene lasts forever. Whole seasons
come and go before it's over and the bear
drops to all fours. Sits down on its
haunches, gives a low, sad growl.
The man puts the tambourine on the table.
Puts the iron bar on the table, too.
Then he takes off his hat. No one
applauds. A few people see
what's coming and walk away. But not
before the hat appears at the edge
of the crowd and begins to make its
way from hand to hand
through the throng. The hat
comes to me and stops. I'm holding
the hat, and I can't believe it.
Everybody staring at it.
I stare right along with them.
You say my name, and in the same breath

hiss, "For God's sake, pass it along."
I toss in the money I have. Then
we leave and go on to the next thing.

Hours later, in bed, I touch you
and wait, and then touch you again.
Whereupon, you uncurl your fingers.
I put my hands all over you then —
your limbs, your long hair even, hair
that I touch and cover my face with,
and draw salt from. But later,
when I close my eyes, the hat
appears. Then the tambourine. The chain.

BLOOD

We were five at the craps table
not counting the croupier
and his assistant. The man
next to me had the dice
cupped in his hand.
He blew on his fingers, said
Come *on*, baby! And leaned
over the table to throw.
At that moment, bright blood rushed
from his nose, spattering
the green felt cloth. He dropped
the dice. Stepped back amazed.
And then terrified as blood
ran down his shirt. God,
what's happening to me?
he cried. Took hold of my arm.
I heard Death's engines turning.
But I was young at the time,
and drunk, and wanted to play.
I didn't have to listen.
So I walked away. Didn't turn back, ever,
or find this in my head, until today.

ALL HER LIFE

I lay down for a nap. But every time I closed my eyes,
mares' tails passed slowly over the Strait
toward Canada. And the waves. They rolled up on the beach
and then back again. You know I don't dream.
But last night I dreamt we were watching
a burial at sea. At first I was astonished.
And then filled with regret. But you
touched my arm and said, "No, it's all right.
She was very old, and he'd loved her all her life."

THE PARTY

Last night, alone, 3000 miles away from the one
I love, I turned the radio on to some jazz
and made a huge bowl of popcorn
with lots of salt on it. Poured butter over it.
Turned out the lights and sat in a chair
in front of the window with the popcorn and
a can of Coke. Forgot everything important
in the world while I ate popcorn and looked out
at a heavy sea, and the lights of town.
The popcorn runny with butter, covered with
salt. I ate it up until there was nothing
left except a few Old Maids. Then
washed my hands. Smoked a couple more cigarettes
while I listened to the beat of the little
music that was left. Things had quieted way down,
though the sea was still running. Wind gave
the house a last shake when I rose
and took three steps, turned, took three more steps, turned.
Then I went to bed and slept wonderfully,
as always. My God, what a life!
But I thought I should explain, leave a note anyhow,
about this mess in the living room
and what went on here last night. Just in case
my lights went out, and I keeled over.
Yes, there was a party here last night.
And the radio's still on. Okay.
But if I die today, I die happy — thinking
of my sweetheart, and of that last popcorn.

INTERVIEW

Talking about myself all day
brought back
something I thought over and
done with. What I'd felt
for Maryann — Anna, she calls
herself now — all those years.

I went to draw a glass of water.
Stood at the window for a time.
When I came back
we passed easily to the next thing.
Went on with my life. But
that memory entering like a spike.

THE COBWEB

A few minutes ago, I stepped onto the deck
of the house. From there I could see and hear the water,
and everything that's happened to me all these years.
It was hot and still. The tide was out.
No birds sang. As I leaned against the railing
a cobweb touched my forehead.
It caught in my hair. No one can blame me that I turned
and went inside. There was no wind. The sea
was dead calm. I hung the cobweb from the lampshade.
Where I watch it shudder now and then when my breath
touches it. A fine thread. Intricate.
Before long, before anyone realizes,
I'll be gone from here.

MARION COHEN

CHILDREN GROW AT NIGHT

Children do not always look cute when they sleep.
Sometimes their foreheads are too high,
The left sides of their lips hang down,
Or their mouths drool wide open
    as they breathe through their noses.
Sometimes the thumbs still glisten from being sucked,
Or an arm dangles off the mattress as though dismembered.
We are not always delighted upon checking on our sleeping children.
We do not always smile with satisfaction in the dark.
After all, it was an unguarded moment when sleep paralyzed their
    bodies,
When they plopped down like little bunny ears,
When the last ounce of consciousness disintegrated.
So don't expect to feel like nodding your head or petting theirs.
And don't be surprised if you see devils rather than angels hovering
    over them,
Or if the music in the background is a dirge rather than a lullaby.
Don't be offended if their limbs twitch at your stare, if the skin
    quivers,
Or if the word they form from their sleep is "help."
Don't be shocked if they snore,
Or if their throats are exposed as though waiting to be cut.
Do not be disappointed if neither their hair nor the covers frames
    their faces,
Or their fingers lie limp between their legs.
And do not be afraid of what lies beneath their eyelids.

TEACHING STURM-LOUVILLE

I multiply the u-equation by v, the v-equation by u, and subtract.
But not enough goes away.
Of course, if I do anything else, none of it goes away.
So I multiply both equations by zero
and then subtract, just in case.

It's all zero.
Circles are zero; ellipses are zero; spheres are zero; R^3 is zero.
The set containing zero is not one but zero.
There is nothing to learn, nothing to teach.
There's been a terrible mistake

WANDA COLEMAN

SOMEWHERE

there's an alley with my name on it
cold gritty pavement
crushed glass
shadows
an occasional thin stray cat
hunting through overturned garbage cans
old tin cans/beer cans/ketchup bottles
cigarette cellophanes
bits of torn paper dancing on an eddy
foot falls stumbling past
lovers in the apartment across the way fucking
argument in the mack den
kids shooting pennies behind crates in back of the liquor store
a few roaches trucking from the fumigated house to the one
across the street
drip drip of water from the drain
wind rises scattering stuff

i will meet you there

UNTITLED

she was the perfect woman
until he discovered she had a mania for flesh
he'd come in late at night. she'd be gnawing away at it under the
    covers

she kept jars of it in the medicine cabinet
and when she kept telling him she had a headache
he would lay there looking at the ceiling, knowing what she was
    really doing

sometimes she'd snatch a bite in public
one day they were visiting mutual friends
she dropped her purse and it fell open
all that red bloody black flesh on the carpet. it was embarrassing
so that night he decided to tell her that it was no good, over,
        finished

and as he mounted the dark stairwell leading to her living quarters
he hesitated. but no, he thought. she loves me

she had crouched behind the door, and as he walked past, she
    sprang

she stored some of the fresh meat in the drawer by her typewriter

she put some chunks of it in the bowl by the bed stand so she could
munch on it while she watched tv
she wrapped the rest of it carefully in tin foil and stuck it in the
    freezer

looking into the mirror she let out something like a bark
well, she thought, i never lie to them. i always tell them what i am.
they never believe me

LUZ

i remember you the way one remembers a bad meal. this evening
you belched up from the memory of a thirteen year old black girl
whose friends were either misfits like herself or belonged to
        another race

i liked you very much luz

enough to maintain our limited friendship though i knew you liked
me less. i was fat, ugly, outcast, the glint in your eye
that hunger that drew me to you was my hunger also

you spoke spanish

used to teach me some and introduce me to your culture, food,
        ways
i knew nothing of illegal aliens but understood your poverty
went deeper than mine. yes, the dimes. i let you steal them from me

you put me down

that was okay, for there was that to which you aspired/the whiteness
of the white world/a door closed and bolted to me
you entered, i remained outside

this night i see your eyes

as clear as if you were here now, your full girlish figure (i had none)
was my envy and has probably gone to fat with many babies or
to dust after many trials. oh luz, i had so many things
to say—so many tight chic referrals to the
latin-black conflicts over white socio-eco crumbs

i wanted to say them through you

all i do remember, think of us/our people as we were
or could have been—apart, the awful silence
together, the awesome storm

BILLY COLLINS

FLAMES

Smokey the Bear heads
into the autumn woods
with a red can of gasoline
and a box of matches.

His hat is cocked
at a disturbing angle.

The moonlight catches the teeth
of his smile.
His paws, the size of catcher's mitts,
crackle into the distance.

He is sick of dispensing
warnings to the careless,
the half-wit camper
the dumbbell hiker.

He is going to show them
how a professional does it.

No one runs after him
with the famous lecture.

EMBRACE

You know the parlor trick.
Wrap your arms around your own torso
and from the back it looks like
someone is embracing you,
her hands tearing at your shirt,
her fingernails teasing your neck.

From the front it is another story.
You never looked so utterly alone,
with your crossed elbows and screwy grin.
You could be waiting for a tailor
to fit you for a straitjacket,
one that would hold you really tight.

THE WILLIES

*"Public restrooms
give me the willies."*
—Ad for a disinfectant

There is no known cure for them,
unlike the heeby-jeebies
or the shakes

which Russian vodka and a hot tub
will smooth out.

The drifties can be licked,
though the vapors often spell trouble.

The whips-and-jangles
go away in time. So do the phantods.
And good company will put the blues
to flight.

But the willies are another matter.

Anything can give them to you:
electric chairs, raw meat, manta rays,
public restrooms, a footprint,
and every case of the willies
is a bad one.

Some say flow with them, ride them out.
But this is useless advice
once you are in their grip.

There is no way to get on top
of the willies. Valium
is ineffective. Hospitals
are not the answer.

Keeping still
and emitting thin, evenly spaced
waves of irony
may help

but don't expect miracles:
the willies are the willies.

GREGORY CORSO

THE WHOLE MESS . . . ALMOST

I ran up six flights of stairs
to my small furnished room
opened the window
and began throwing out
those things most important in life

First to go, Truth, squealing like a fink:
"Don't! I'll tell awful things about you!"
"Oh yeah? Well, I've nothing to hide . . . OUT!"
Then went God, glowering & whimpering in amazement:
      "It's not my fault! I'm not the cause of it all!" "OUT!"

Then Love, cooing bribes: "You'll never know impotency!
All the girls on *Vogue* covers, all yours!"
I pushed her fat ass out and screamed:
"You always end up a bummer!"
I picked up Faith Hope Charity
all three clinging together:
"Without us you'll surely die!"
"With you I'm going nuts! Goodbye!"

Then Beauty . . . ah, Beauty —
As I led her to the window
I told her: "You I loved best in life
. . . but you're a killer; Beauty kills!"
Not really meaning to drop her
I immediately ran downstairs
getting there just in time to catch her
"You saved me!" she cried
I put her down and told her: "Move on."
Went back up those six flights
went to the money
there was no money to throw out.
The only thing left in the room was Death
hiding beneath the kitchen sink:
"I'm not real!" It cried
"I'm just a rumor spread by life . . ."
Laughing I threw it out, kitchen sink and all
and suddenly realized Humor
was all that was left —
All I could do with Humor was to say:
"Out the window with the window!"

THE MAD YAK

I am watching them churn the last milk
    they'll ever get from me.
They are waiting for me to die;
They want to make buttons out of my bones.
Where are my sisters and brothers?
That tall monk there, loading my uncle,
    he has a new cap.
And that idiot student of his —
    I never saw that muffler before.
Poor uncle, he lets them load him.
How sad he is, how tired!
I wonder what they'll do with his bones?
And that beautiful tail!
How many shoelaces will they make of that!

ON THE WALLS OF A DULL
FURNISHED ROOM . . .

I hang old photos of my childhood girls —
With breaking heart I sit, elbow on table,
Chin on hand, studying
    the proud eyes of Helen,
    the weak mouth of Jane,
    the golden hair of Susan.

ITALIAN EXTRAVAGANZA

Mrs. Lombardi's month-old son is dead.
I saw it in Rizzo's funeral parlor,
A small purplish wrinkled head.

They've just finished having high mass for it;
They're coming out now
. . .wow, such a small coffin!
And ten black cadillacs to haul it in.

JAYNE CORTEZ

RAPE

What was Inez supposed to do for
the man who declared war on her body
the man who carved a combat zone between her
breasts
Was she supposed to lick crabs from his hairy ass
kiss every pimple on his butt
blow hot breath on his big toe
draw back the corners of her vagina and
hee haw like a California burro

This being war time for Inez
she stood facing the knife
the insults and
her own smell drying on the penis of
the man who raped her

She stood with a rifle in her hand
doing what a defense department will do in times of war
And when the man started grunting and panting and wobbling
    forward like
a giant hog
She pumped lead into his three hundred pounds of shaking flesh
Sent it flying to the Virgin of Guadalupe
then celebrated the day of the dead rapist punk
and just what the fuck else was she supposed to do?

And what was Joanne supposed to do for
the man who declared war on her life
Was she supposed to tongue his encrusted
toilet stool lips
suck the numbers off of his tin badge
choke on his clap trap balls
squeeze on his nub of rotten maggots and
sing god bless america thank you for fucking my life away

This being wartime for Joanne
she did what a defense department will do in times of war
and when the piss drinking   shit sniffing guard said
I'm gonna make you wish you were dead black bitch
come here
Joanne came down with an ice pick in
the swat freak motherfucker's chest
yes in the fat neck of that racist policeman
Joanne did the dance of the ice picks and once again
from coast to coast
house to house
we celebrated day of the dead rapist punk
and just what the fuck else were we supposed to do

THEY CAME AGAIN IN 1970 IN 1980

You didn't send for them
but in the name of god and progress
they came again
Missionaries and scientists arriving
with television sets and microwave ovens
Military advisors landing
with a party of born-again puritans
Bible societies blowing in
with a battery of translators
Bankers coming with loans
with indian-head nickels
Bulldozers entering the undergrowth
from two points in the river
Death exchanging drinks
at the first whiff of petroleum
And in the name of god & progress &
stuffed pockets
after so much torture
& so many invasions in the blood
your veins   are
air strips for
multi-national corporations
Your native sweat is
aviation fuel for
drilling rigs
Your compound is like
a French Devil's Island
And when the eagle flies through
the Amazon rain forest on friday
everything falls into
the pulp of the ferment of your lips
to kiss the landscape goodbye

I SEE CHANO POZO

A very fine conga of sweat
a very fine stomp of the right foot
a very fine platform of sticks
a very fine tube of frictional groans
a very fine can of belligerent growls
a very fine hoop of cubano yells
very fine   very fine

Is there anyone finer today   olé   okay
Oye   I say
I see Chano Pozo
Chano Pozo from Havana Cuba
                    You're the one
You're the one who made Atamo into
a tattooed motivator of revolutionary spirits

You're the one who made Mpebi into
an activated slasher of lies

You're the one who made Donno into
an armpit of inflammable explosives

You're the one who made Obonu into
a circle of signifying snakes

You're the one who made Atumpan's head strike
against
the head of a bird   everynight   everyday
in your crisscrossing chant
in your cross river mouth
                    You're the one
Oye   I say
Chano
what made you roar like a big brazos flood
what made you yodel like a migrating frog
what made you shake like atomic heat
what made you jell into a ritual pose
Chano   Chano   Chano
what made your technology of thumps so new so
mean
I say
is there anyone meaner than Chano Pozo
                    from Havana Cuba

Oye
I'm in the presence of ancestor
                    Chano Pozo
Chano connector of two worlds
You go and celebrate again with
the *compañeros* in Santiago
   and tell us about it
You go to the spirit house of Antonio Maceo
and tell us about it
You go to Angola
and tell us about it
You go to Calabar
and tell us about it
You go see the slave castles
you go see the massacres
you go see the afflictions
you go see the battlefields
you go see the warriors
you go as a healer
you go conjurate
you go mediate
you go to the cemetery of drums
return and tell us about it

Lucumi   Abakwa   Lucumi   Abakwa

Olé   okay
Is there anyone finer today
Oye   I say
did you hear
Mpintintoa smoking in the palm of his hands
did you hear
Ilya Ilu booming through the cup of his clap
did you hear
Ntenga sanding on the rim of his rasp
did you hear
Siky Akkua stuttering like a goat sucking hawk
did you hear
Bata crying in a nago tongue
did you hear
Fontomfrom speaking through the skull of a dog

did you hear it   did you hear it   did you hear it

A very fine tree stump of drones
a very fine shuffle of shrines
a very fine turn of the head
a very fine tissue of skin
a very fine smack of the lips
a very fine pulse
a very fine *encuentro*
very fine   very fine   very fine
Is there anyone finer than
Chano Pozo from Havana Cuba
Oye   I say
I see Chano Pozo

DIANE DI PRIMA

THE JOURNEY

from *New Mexico Poem*

The city I want to visit is made of porcelain
The dead are gathered there, they are at their best:
Bob Thompson
in his checkered jacket & little hat, his grin
full of cocaine, spinning down the street; Frank drunk
spitting out tales of Roussel, of Mayakovsky
brief anecdotes over bacon and eggs on a roll,
his keenness against the wind; Fred in pointed shoes
drinking an egg cream, his leotard over his shoulder
in a little bag, waving amphetamine hands at the sky

The porcelain city glitters, I feel my friends
hastening to join it & to join me there:
Bob Creeley tearing through Buffalo streets seeking entry
John Wieners holding still, mumbling and waiting
tears under his eyelids; I walk in that brittle city
still sleepy and arrogant and desperately in love . . .

BIOLOGY LESSON

It's sinister how everything comes alive
in the summer: on my light-table now,
    one small flea-like creature, doing backwards jumps
    one flat thing looking rather like a date-pit
    with legs; one fly (?) with strip-ed wings

downstairs the compost garbage grows pink mold
every night, over whatever I threw away
the day before: weird smell, too; if I leave the cornmeal open
a field mouse, or equally tiny creature leaves droppings
on its top, after eating a gigantic meal

something lives in the wall of my bedroom, is never home
except on rare occasions (rainy nights)
the whole place practically crawls
    the green moist chilly warmth yin air
    busy as hell, the whole thing coming together
all over the place

they were dead wrong about no spontaneous
generation

LETTER TO JEANNE (at Tassajara)

dry heat of the Tassajara canyon
moist warmth of San Francisco summer
bright fog reflecting sunrise as you
step out of September zendo
heart of your warmth, my girl, as you step out
into your vajra pathway, glinting
like your eyes turned sideways at us
your high knowing 13-year-old
wench-smile, flicking your thin
ankles you trot toward Adventure
all sizes & shapes, O may it be various
for you as for me it was, sparkle
like dustmotes at dawn in the back
of grey stores, like the shooting stars
over the Hudson, wind in the Berkshire pines

O you have landscapes dramatic like mine
never was, uncounted caves
to mate in, my scorpio, bright love
like fire light up your beauty years
on these new, jagged hills

NOTE TO ROI

from *Ode to Keats*

I wonder often what it is that you are doing —
How much of it *is* pride, or ambition
As we so easily say.
I remember the message I gave Freddie for you
That I would see you again at the end of this
(Meaning my marriage and yours)
Not dreaming how far that would take us:
Freddie dead —
You living in Harlem, where you'll surely be killed
Gunned down, like Malcolm X, in some hotel
Or haberdasher's shop — some bleak room or street
Without my having told you you were my love
Among the adventures & common sense of my life.

STEPHEN DOBYNS

CREEPING INTELLIGENCE

Two men take three party girls to a motel.
All night long they imitate the shapes
of a dozen different kinds of pretzels.
In the morning, one man has a crick in his back.
He can't straighten up. Goodbye, goodbye,
say the girls. His friend goes off to work.
The man still can't straighten up. He had been
well over six feet tall and now he's bent down
to little more than a yard. The whole world
looks different. He hobbles along the street
staring into people's stomachs, eye to eye
with big dogs, at chin level with the hood
ornaments of expensive cars. This was a man
who knew all the answers, who could lecture
nonstop about bald spots and eyebrows.
Now he stares up into men's beards. Breasts
loom heavily above him. What a fool I was,
he cries. Humility slaps him across the face.
He decides he must tell people of his new view
of the world so he drags a soapbox to the park
and climbs up on top. A crowd gathers.
Immediately he is again over six feet tall.
A sea of bald spots spreads beneath him.
He forgets what he wanted to say, something
about the sin of pride. People clap their hands.
The man sings every Stephen Foster song
he can remember. Then he does a little dance.
The crowd continues to clap. The man grows
so excited that he falls off the soapbox.
When he gets to his feet, he finds he can
again straighten up. Whew, what a close call.
No more party girls for him. He goes home
to his wife. Domestic bliss. In the evening
they sit before the fire and his wife knits.
The man stares at the flames and feels he has forgotten
something important. Clunk, clunk, goes his brain.
The man busts half his gray cells before he stops.
Why bother? he thinks: Life is hard enough.
Later he slaps his wife on the rump. Come on,
old horse, time for another turn in the saddle.
They go to bed. In the very act of making love,
the man has a vision of himself in a space capsule
orbiting the earth. Through the little window
he can see other capsules with other people
but they can't talk, they can only wave. They get
gradually smaller until they shrink down
to black spots on a black horizon and the man
is alone staring into the infinite night.
Then he has his orgasm and pulls out.

Goodbye, goodbye, he says to the darkness.
You know, he tells his wife, somehow it's sad.
But he can't decide what's sad or why or for how long,
or how to break free of the riddle he inhabits.
Sometimes it happens like this. Knocked off his feet
by midnight depression. He's been working too hard.
He must push aside these nagging worries. Luckily,
he knows a couple of girls. He'll invite them
to a motel — night of sexual abandon. Party girls,
where would the world be without party girls?
Time's passing, he thinks, you only live once.

WHITE PIG

A family decides to have a party.
It is a graduation or birthday.
The father buys a little white pig,
just enough for his wife and six kids
with something left over for someone special.
The father has no idea how to kill a pig
but he meets a man in a bar who says,
Don't worry, I have killed hundreds of pigs.
He is a young man with a big smile.
On the day of the party, the young man arrives
early in the morning. I have no knife,
he says. And he takes the bread knife
and begins sharpening it on a stone.
He sharpens the knife and drinks brandy.
The white pig trots through the house.
The children have tied a blue ribbon
around her neck and the baby's blue bonnet
on her head. The pig thinks she is very cute.
She lets the children feed her cookies and
ride on her back. The man with the smile keeps
sharpening and drinking, sharpening and drinking.
The morning is getting late. Why don't you
do something? says the father. The pig pokes
her head around the door, then scampers away.
The young man drinks more brandy. It is nearly noon.
Why don't you kill the pig? says the father.
He wants to get it over with. The young man
looks sullenly at the floor, looks sullenly
at the father and his neat little house.
He gets to his feet and sways back and forth.
You're drunk, says the father. The young man
raises the knife. Not too drunk to kill a pig,
he shouts. He stumbles out of the kitchen.
Where's that bitch of a pig? he shouts.
The pig is upstairs with the children.
I'm ready, says the young man, now I'm
really ready. He rushes up the stairs
and into the room where the pig is playing.
You whore! he shouts. He dives at the pig
and stabs her in the leg. The pig squeals.

Outside, shouts the father, you have to kill her
outside! The pig is terrified and rushes
around the room squealing and bleeding on the rug.
The blue bonnet slips down over one eye.
You slut! shouts the young man. He leaps
at the pig and stabs her in the shoulder.
The children are screaming. The father is shouting.
The young man chases the pig through the whole house.
You whore, you slut, you little Jew of a pig!
Outside, outside! shouts the father. He knows
the rules, knows how a pig should be killed.
For the pig, it's a nightmare. The blue bonnet
has slipped down over both eyes and she can
hardly see. She squeals over and over. There is
no sound in the world like that one.
It's a sound like hot grease in your face.
At last the young man traps the pig
in the laundry room. He leaps on her.
You black bitch of a pig! he shouts. He stabs
the pig over and over. The children
stand in the doorway crying. The father
is crying. His wife hides in the bedroom.
What a great party this has turned out to be.
Finally the pig is dead. The young man
holds her up by the hind legs. Again he is
smiling. This is one dead pig! he shouts.
He has probably stabbed her over two hundred times.
The pig looks like a piece of Swiss cheese.
The young man carries the pig to the kitchen
and begins to butcher her, then he helps
to cook the pig. All afternoon the house
is full of wonderful smells. The children
hide in their bedrooms. The mother and father
scrub and scrub to clean up the blood. At last
the pig is ready to be eaten. It is a party,
maybe a graduation or birthday.
The children refuse to come downstairs.
The mother and father don't feel hungry.
The young man sits at the table by himself.
He is served by a neighborhood girl hired
to wash the dishes. He eats and eats. Tasty,
he says, there's nothing so tasty as young pig.
He drinks wine and laughs. He stuffs himself
on the sweet flesh of the little white pig.
Late at night he is still eating. The children
are in bed, the parents are in bed. The father
lies on his back and listens to the young man singing—
hunting songs, marching songs, songs of journeys
through dark places, songs of conquest and revenge.

LAURIE DUESING

THE VALLEY LOUNGE

I'm the sober one, the one who answered the telephone
just as the band in this bar began to set up,
a woman no longer alone but with the tall blond man,
the one the old lady on the end stool says
has been keeping them in stitches for an hour,

the same man whose left arm is draped over the shoulder
of his best friend's girl. You know the gesture,
the kind men tell you means nothing,
as if arms and shoulders are interchangeable
and only flesh below the nipple line counts.

I'm the woman who came three hours late,
who can't catch up, whose shoulders
are now draped by the tall blond's arms.
I love him, and the love does not change which tells me
about love's hardness which is no less hard than the faces

of the women sitting on stools who are probably younger
than I am, and despite the set of their faces, think something soft
could still happen to them. Not here, I think,
watching them fidget like adolescent girls on important birthdays
who are given lipstick because they were too embarrassed

to admit they wanted a doll, which is what I hear
one of them call the male stripper — a living doll —
a man wearing a cowboy hat and bandana
who dry humps the women. Soft where the women are hard,
his face is smooth: mouth, rouged. He strips
to a gold jock strap, his crotch snaking in front
of a woman's mouth. When her tongue pokes between her lips,
the man behind her, in hope of spillover,
puts his hand on her shoulder
                                              as a hand slides

over my eyes and my fiancé says, "Don't look.
Don't look. You're the kind of girl men marry."
But through fingers I see the stripper is down
to a leopard skin G-string covering a groin
as flat as dreams which have lost their air.

Everything begins to fall: the women's faces, my fiancé's hand
from my eyes to my side, a hand I now hold harder
than any desire I've known and with the same urgency
as everyone else in this bar, all of us waiting
to catch what someone else drops.

A MIRACLE

After you'd been killed, you often walked up
behind me and rested your hands on my shoulders
That was no miracle. Neither was the fact I'd catch
you in peripheral glance pacing the living room,
your right arm crooked over your head,
fingers raking your thick dark hair.
Nor the mornings I found the garage door open
your tools rearranged on the cement floor.
I knew you'd never leave me, something the physician
who would not let me hold your dead hand
failed to understand. He was trying to separate
the living woman from the dead man and did not know
the living and the dead never let go.
Simply because they don't have to.
So when I lift your green T-shirt from the drawer
to feel your body's smells or when you speak
to me in my dreams, never think I am ungrateful.
But even with the sweetness of nothing, flesh longs
for its kind. The next time your spirit walks
the house, if you'd stop, hold still
and let me come to you, hold your hand in mine,
that, my love, would be a miracle.

beatify

LAWRENCE FERLINGHETTI

City Lights Bookstore in S.F.

THE LOVE NUT

I go into the men's room Springfield bus station
on the way back to Muhlenberg County
and see this nut in the mirror
Who let in this weirdo Who let in this creep?
He's the kind writes I LOVE YOU on toilet walls and wants to
    embrace everybody in the lobby He writes his phone number
    inside a heart on the wall He's some kinda pervert Mister Eros
    the Great Lover
He wants to run up to everybody in the waiting room and kiss them
    on the spot and say Why aren't we friends and lovers Can I go
    home with you You got anything to drink or smoke Let's you
    and me get together The time is now or sooner
He wants to take all the stray dogs and cats and people home with
    him and turn them on to making love all the time wherever
He wants to scatter poems from airplanes across the landscape He's
    some kinda poetic nut Like he thinks he's Dylan Thomas and
    Bob Dylan rolled together with Charlie Chaplin thrown in
He wants to lip-read everybody's thoughts and feelings and longings
    He's a dangerous nut He's gotta be insane He has no sense of
    sin
He wants to heat up all the dead-looking people the unhappy-
    looking people in bus stations and airports He wants to heat up
    their beds He wants to open their bodies and heads
He's some kinda airhead rolling stone He don't wanna be alone He
    may be queer on men
He's the kind addresses everybody on buses making them laugh and
    look away and then look back again
He wants to get everyone to burst out laughing and sighing and
    crying and singing and dancing and kissing each other
    including old ladies and policemen
He's gotta be mad He's so glad to be alive he's real strange He's got
    the hots for humanity one at a time He wants to kiss your
    breasts He wants to lie still between them singing in a low voice
He wants everyone to lie down together and roll around together
    moaning and singing and having visions and orgasms He wants
    to come in you He wants you to come with him He wants us all
    to come together One hot world One heartbeat
He wants he wants us all to lie down together in Paradise in the
    Garden of Love in the Garden of Delights and couple together
    like a train a chain-reaction a chain-letter-of-love around the
    world on hot nights
He wants he wants he wants! He's gotta be crazy Call the cops Take
    him away!

TWO SCAVENGERS IN A TRUCK, TWO BEAUTIFUL PEOPLE IN A MERCEDES

At the stoplight waiting for the light
                  Nine A.M. downtown San Francisco
a bright yellow garbage truck
          with two garbagemen in red plastic blazers
standing on the back stoop
             one on each side hanging on
and looking down into
             an elegant open Mercedes
  with an elegant couple in it
The man
    in a hip three-piece linen suit
      with shoulder-length blond hair & sunglasses
The young blond woman so casually coifed
        with a short skirt and colored stockings
  on the way to his architect's office

And the two scavengers up since Four A.M.
            grungy from their route
The older of the two with grey iron hair
        and hunched back
    looking down like some
           gargoyle Quasimodo
And the younger of the two
         also with sunglasses & longhair
  about the same age as the Mercedes driver

And both scavengers gazing down
           as from a great distance
    at the cool couple
as if they were watching some odorless TV ad
        in which everything is always possible

And the very red light for an instant
        holding all four close together
  as if anything at all were possible
           between them
  across that great gulf
            in the high seas
                of this democracy

EDWARD FIELD

political

DONKEYS

They are not silent like workhorses
Who are happy or indifferent about the plow and wagon;
Donkeys don't submit like that
For they are sensitive
And cry continually under their burdens:
Yes, they are animals of sensibility
Even if they aren't intelligent enough
To count money or discuss religion.

Laugh if you will when they heehaw
But know that they are crying
When they make that noise that sounds like something
Between a squawking water pump and a foghorn.

And when I hear them sobbing
I suddenly notice their sweet eyes and ridiculous ears
And their naive bodies that look as though they never grew up
But stayed children, as in fact they are;
And being misunderstood as children are
They are forced to walk up mountains
With men and bundles on their backs.

Somehow I am glad that they do not submit without a protest
But as their masters are of the deafest
The wails are never heard.

I am sure that donkeys know what life should be
But, alas, they do not own their bodies;
And if they had their own way, I am sure
That they would sit in a field of flowers
Kissing each other, and maybe
They would even invite us to join them.

For they never let us forget that they know
(As everyone knows who stays as sweet as children)
That there is a far better way to spend time;
You can be sure of that when they stop in their tracks
And honk and honk and honk.

And if I tried to explain to them
Why work is not only necessary but good,
I am afraid that they would never understand
And kick me with their back legs
As commentary on my wisdom.

So they remain unhappy and sob
And their masters who are equally convinced of being right
Beat them and hear nothing.

A JOURNEY

When he got up that morning everything was different:
He enjoyed the bright spring day
But he did not realize it exactly, he just enjoyed it.

And walking down the street to the railroad station
Past magnolia trees with dying flowers like old socks
It was a long time since he had breathed so simply.

Tears filled his eyes and it felt good
But he held them back
Because men didn't walk around crying in that town.

And waiting on the platform at the station
The fear came over him of something terrible about to happen:
The train was late and he recited the alphabet to keep hold.

And in its time it came screeching in
And as it went on making its usual stops,
People coming and going, telephone poles passing,

He hid his head behind a newspaper
No longer able to hold back the sobs, and willed his eyes
To follow the rational weavings of the seat fabric.

He didn't do anything violent as he had imagined.
He cried for a long time, but when he finally quieted down
A place in him that had been closed like a fist was open,

And at the end of the ride he stood up and got off that train:
And through the streets and in all the places he lived in later on
He walked, himself at last, a man among men,
With such radiance that everyone looked up and wondered.

WORLD WAR II

It was over Target Berlin the flak shot up our plane
just as we were dumping bombs on the already smoking city
on signal from the lead bomber in the squadron.
The plane jumped again and again as the shells burst under us
sending jagged pieces of steel rattling through our fuselage.
I'll never understand
how none of us got ripped by those fragments.

Then, being hit, we had to drop out of formation right away
losing speed and altitude,
and when I figured out our course with trembling hands on the
    instruments
(I was navigator)
we set out on the long trip home to England
alone, with two of our four engines gone
and gas streaming out of holes in the wing tanks.
That morning at briefing
we had been warned not to go to nearby Poland
partly liberated then by the Russians,
although later we learned that another crew in trouble
had landed there anyway,
and patching up their plane somehow,
returned gradually to England

roundabout by way of Turkey and North Africa.
But we chose England, and luckily
the Germans had no fighters to send up after us then
for this was just before they developed their jet.
To lighten our load we threw out
guns and ammunition, my navigation books, all the junk
and made it over Holland
with a few goodbye fireworks from the shore guns.

Over the North Sea the third engine gave out
and we dropped low over the water.
The gas gauge read empty but by keeping the nose down
a little gas at the bottom of the tank sloshed forward
and kept our single engine going.
High overhead, the squadrons were flying home in formation—
the raids had gone on for hours after us.
Did they see us down there in our trouble?
We radioed our final position for help to come
but had no idea if anyone
happened to be tuned in and heard us,
and we crouched together on the floor
knees drawn up and head down
in regulation position for ditching;
listened as the engine stopped, a terrible silence,
and we went down into the sea with a crash,
just like hitting a brick wall,
jarring bones, teeth, eyeballs panicky.
Who would ever think water could be so hard?
You black out, and then come to
with water rushing in like a sinking-ship movie.

All ten of us started getting out of there fast:
There was a convenient door in the roof to climb out by,
one at a time. We stood in line,
water up to our thighs and rising.
The plane was supposed to float for twenty seconds
but with all those flak holes
who could say how long it really would?
The two life rafts popped out of the sides into the water
but one of them only half inflated
and the other couldn't hold everyone
although they all piled into it, except the pilot,
who got into the limp raft that just floated.
The radio operator and I, out last,
(Did that mean we were least aggressive, least likely to survive?)
we stood on the wing watching the two rafts
being swept off by waves in different directions.
We had to swim for it.
Later they said the cords holding rafts to plane
broke by themselves, but I wouldn't have blamed them
for cutting them loose, for fear
that by waiting the plane would go down
and drag them with it.

I headed for the overcrowded raft
and after a clumsy swim in soaked heavy flying clothes
got there and hung onto the side.
The radio operator went for the half-inflated raft
where the pilot lay with water sloshing over him,
but he couldn't swim, even with his life vest on,
being from the Great Plains—
his strong farmer's body didn't know

how to wallow through water properly
and a wild current seemed to sweep him farther off.
One minute we saw him on top of a swell
and perhaps we glanced away for a minute
but when we looked again he was gone—
just as the plane went down sometime around then
when nobody was looking.

It was midwinter and the waves were mountains
and the water ice water.
You could live in it twenty-five minutes
the Ditching Survival Manual said.
Since most of the crew were squeezed on my raft
I had to stay in the water hanging on.
My raft? It was their raft, they got there first so they would live.
Twenty-five minutes I had.
Live, live, I said to myself.
You've got to live.
There looked like plenty of room on the raft
from where I was and I said so
but they said no.
When I figured the twenty-five minutes were about up
and I was getting numb,
I said I couldn't hold on anymore,
and a little rat-faced boy from Alabama, one of the gunners,
got into the icy water in my place,
and I got on the raft in his.
He insisted on taking off his flying clothes
which was probably his downfall because even wet clothes are
    protection,
and then worked hard, kicking with his legs, and we all paddled,
to get to the other raft,
and we tied them together.
The gunner got in the raft with the pilot
and lay in the wet.
Shortly after, the pilot started gurgling green foam from his
    mouth—
maybe he was injured in the crash against the instruments—
and by the time we were rescued,
he and the little gunner were both dead.

That boy who took my place in the water
who died instead of me
I don't remember his name even.
It was like those who survived the death camps
by letting others go into the ovens in their place.
It was him or me, and I made up my mind to live.
I'm a good swimmer,
but I didn't swim off in that scary sea
looking for the radio operator when he was washed away.
I suppose, then, once and for all,
I chose to live rather than be a hero, as I still do today,
although at that time I believed in being heroic, in saving the world,
even if, when opportunity knocked,
I instinctively chose survival.

As evening fell the waves calmed down
and we spotted a boat, far off, and signaled with a flare gun,
hoping it was English not German.
The only two who cried on being found
were me and a boy from Boston, a gunner.
The rest of the crew kept straight faces.

It was a British air-sea rescue boat:
They hoisted us up on deck,
dried off the living and gave us whisky and put us to bed,
and rolled the dead up in blankets,
and delivered us all to a hospital on shore
for treatment or disposal.
None of us even caught cold, only the dead.

This was a minor accident of war;
Two weeks in a rest camp at Southport on the Irish Sea
and we were back at Grafton-Underwood, our base,
ready for combat again,
the dead crewmen replaced by living ones,
and went on hauling bombs over the continent of Europe,
destroying the Germans and their cities.

THE FAREWELL

They say the ice will hold
so there I go,
forced to believe them by my act of trusting people,
stepping out on it,

and naturally it gaps open
and I, forced to carry on coolly
by my act of being imperturbable,
slide erectly into the water wearing my captain's helmet,
waving to the shore with a sad smile,
"Goodbye my darlings, goodbye dear one,"
as the ice meets again over my head with a click.

ALLEN GINSBERG

DREAM RECORD: JUNE 8, 1955

A drunken night in my house with a
boy, San Francisco: I lay asleep:
darkness:
        I went back to Mexico City
and saw Joan Burroughs leaning
forward in a garden chair, arms
on her knees. She studied me with
clear eyes and downcast smile, her
face restored to a fine beauty
tequila and salt had made strange
before the bullet in her brow.

We talked of the life since then.
Well, what's Burroughs doing now?
Bill on earth, he's in North Africa.
Oh, and Kerouac? Jack still jumps
with the same beat genius as before,
notebooks filled with Buddha.
I hope he makes it, she laughed.
Is Huncke still in the can? No,
last time I saw him on Times Square.
And how is Kenney? Married, drunk
and golden in the East. You? New
loves in the West—
        Then I knew
she was a dream: and questioned her.
—Joan, what kind of knowledge have
the dead? can you still love
your mortal acquaintances?
What do you remember of us?
        She
faded in front of me— The next instant
I saw her rain-stained tombstone
rear an illegible epitaph
under the gnarled branch of a small
tree in the wild grass
of an unvisited garden in Mexico.

DEATH TO VAN GOGH'S EAR! ← Political

POET is Priest
Money has reckoned the soul of America
Congress broken thru to the precipice of Eternity
the President built a War machine which will vomit and rear up Russia
　　out of Kansas
The American Century betrayed by a mad Senate which no longer
　　sleeps with its wife
Franco has murdered Lorca the fairy son of Whitman
just as Mayakovsky committed suicide to avoid Russia
Hart Crane distinguished Platonist committed suicide to cave in the
　　wrong America
just as millions of tons of human wheat were burned in secret caverns
　　under the White House
while India starved and screamed and ate mad dogs full of rain
and mountains of eggs were reduced to white powder in the halls of
　　Congress
no godfearing man will walk there again because of the stink of the
　　rotten eggs of America
and the Indians of Chiapas will continue to gnaw their vitaminless
　　tortillas
aborigines of Australia perhaps gibber in the eggless wilderness
and I rarely have an egg for breakfast tho my work requires infinite eggs
　　to come to birth in Eternity
eggs should be eaten or given to their mothers
and the grief of the countless chickens of America is expressed in the
　　screaming of her comedians over the radio
Detroit has built a million automobiles of rubber trees and phantoms
but I walk, I walk, and the Orient walks with me, and all Africa walks
and sooner or later North America will walk
for as we have driven the Chinese Angel from our door he will drive us
　　from the Golden Door of the future
we have not cherished pity on Tanganyika
Einstein alive was mocked for his heavenly politics
Bertrand Russell driven from New York for getting laid
immortal Chaplin driven from our shores with the rose in his teeth
a secret conspiracy by Catholic Church in the lavatories of Congress
　　has denied contraceptives to the unceasing masses of India.
Nobody publishes a word that is not the cowardly robot ravings of a
　　depraved mentality
The day of the publication of the true literature of the American body
　　will be day of Revolution
the revolution of the sexy lamb
the only bloodless revolution that gives away corn
poor Genet will illuminate the harvesters of Ohio
Marijuana is a benevolent narcotic but J. Edgar Hoover prefers his
　　deathly scotch
And the heroin of Lao-Tze & the Sixth Patriarch is punished by the
　　electric chair
but the poor sick junkies have nowhere to lay their heads
fiends in our government have invented a cold-turkey cure for addiction
　　as obsolete as the Defense Early Warning Radar System
I am the defense early warning radar system
I see nothing but bombs
I am not interested in preventing Asia from being Asia
and the governments of Russia and Asia will rise and fall but Asia and
　　Russia will not fall
the government of America also will fall but how can America fall
I doubt if anyone will ever fall anymore except governments
fortunately all the governments will fall

61

the only ones which won't fall are the good ones
and the good ones don't yet exist
But they have to begin existing they exist in my poems
they exist in the death of the Russian and American governments
they exist in the death of Hart Crane & Mayakovsky
Now is the time for prophecy without death as a consequence
the universe will ultimately disappear
Hollywood will rot on the windmills of Eternity
Hollywood whose movies stick in the throat of God
Yes Hollywood will get what it deserves
Time
Seepage of nerve-gas over the radio
History will make this poem prophetic and its awful silliness a hideous
    spiritual music
I have the moan of doves and the feather of ecstasy
Man cannot long endure the hunger of the cannibal abstract
War is abstract
the world will be destroyed
but I will die only for poetry, that will save the world
Monument to Sacco & Vanzetti not yet financed to ennoble Boston
natives of Kenya tormented by idiot con-men from England
South Africa in the grip of the white fool
Vachel Lindsay Secretary of the Interior
Poe Secretary of Imagination
Pound Secty. Economics
and Kra belongs to Kra, and Pukti to Pukti
crossfertilization of Blok and Artaud
Van Gogh's Ear on the currency
no more propaganda for monsters
and poets should stay out of politics or become monsters
I have become monstrous with politics
the Russian poet undoubtedly monstrous in his secret notebook
Tibet should be left alone
These are obvious prophecies
America will be destroyed
Russian poets will struggle with Russia
Whitman warned against this "fabled Damned of nations"
Where was Theodore Roosevelt when he sent out ultimatums from his
    castle in Camden
Where was the House of Representatives when Crane read aloud from
    his prophetic books
What was Wall Street scheming when Lindsay announced the doom of
    Money
Were they listening to my ravings in the locker rooms of Bickfords Em-
    ployment Offices?
Did they bend their ears to the moans of my soul when I struggled with
    market research statistics in the Forum at Rome?
No they were fighting in fiery offices, on carpets of heartfailure, scream-
    ing and bargaining with Destiny
fighting the Skeleton with sabers, muskets, buck teeth, indigestion,
    bombs of larceny, whoredom, rockets, pederasty,
back to the wall to build up their wives and apartments, lawns, suburbs,
    fairydoms,
Puerto Ricans crowded for massacre on 114th St. for the sake of an
    imitation Chinese-Moderne refrigerator
Elephants of mercy murdered for the sake of an Elizabethan birdcage
millions of agitated fanatics in the bughouse for the sake of the scream-
    ing soprano of industry
Money-chant of soapers — toothpaste apes in television sets —
    deodorizers on hypnotic chairs —

petroleum mongers in Texas — jet plane streaks among the clouds —
sky writers liars in the face of Divinity — fanged butchers of hats and
    shoes,
all Owners! Owners! Owners! with obsession on property and vanish-
    ing Selfhood!
and their long editorials on the fence of the screaming negro attacked
    by ants crawled out of the front page!
Machinery of a mass electrical dream! A war-creating Whore of Baby-
    lon bellowing over Capitols and Academies!
Money! Money! Money! shrieking mad celestial money of illusion!
    Money made of nothing, starvation, suicide! Money of failure!
    Money of death!
Money against Eternity! and eternity's strong mills grind out vast
    paper of Illusion!

Paris, December 1957

TO LINDSAY

Vachel, the stars are out
dusk has fallen on the Colorado road
a car crawls slowly across the plain
in the dim light the radio blares its jazz
the heartbroken salesman lights another cigarette
In another city 27 years ago
I see your shadow on the wall
you're sitting in your suspenders on the bed
the shadow hand lifts up a Lysol bottle to your head
your shade falls over on the floor

Paris, May 1958

OVER DENVER AGAIN

Gray clouds blot sunglare, mountains float west, plane
softly roaring over Denver — Neal dead a year — clean suburb
    yards,
fit boardinghouse for the homosexual messenger's
alleyway Lila a decade back before the Atombomb.
Denver without Neal, eh? Denver with orange sunsets
& giant airplanes winging silvery to San Francisco —
watchtowers in red cold planet light, when the Earth Angel's dead
the dead material planet'll revolve robotlike
& insects hop back and forth between metallic cities.

February 13, 1969

RAIN-WET ASPHALT HEAT, GARBAGE CURBED CANS OVERFLOWING

I hauled down lifeless mattresses to sidewalk refuse-piles,
old rugs stept on from Paterson to Lower East Side filled with bed-
    bugs,
gray pillows, couch seats treasured from the street laid back on the
    street
— out, to hear Murder-tale, 3rd Street cyclists attacked tonite —
Bopping along in rain, Chaos fallen over City roofs,
shrouds of chemical vapour drifting over building-tops —
Get The *Times*, Nixon says peace reflected from the Moon,
but I found no boy body to sleep with all night on pavements 3 A.M.
    home in sweating drizzle —
Those mattresses soggy lying by full five garbagepails —
Barbara, Maretta, Peter Steven Rosebud slept on these Pillows years
    ago,
forgotten names, also made love to me, I had these mattresses four
    years on my floor —
Gerard, Jimmy, many months, even blond Gordon later,
Paul with the beautiful big cock, that teenage boy that lived in
    Pennsylvania,
forgotten numbers, young dream loves and lovers, earthly bellies —
many strong youths with eyes closed, come sighing and helping me
    come —
Desires already forgotten, tender persons used and kissed goodbye
and all the times I came to myself alone in the dark dreaming of
    Neal or Billy Budd
— nameless angels of half-life — heart beating & eyes weeping for
    lovely phantoms —
Back from the Gem Spa, into the hallway, a glance behind
and sudden farewell to the bedbug-ridden mattresses piled soggy in
    dark rain.

August 2, 1969

"WHAT WOULD YOU DO IF YOU LOST IT?"

said Rinpoche Chögyam Trungpa Tulku in the marble glittering apart-
    ment lobby
looking at my black hand-box full of Art, "Better prepare for
    Death" . . .
The harmonium that's Peter's
the scarf that's Krishna's the bell and brass lightningbolt Phil Whalen
    selected in Japan
a tattered copy of Blake, with chord notations, black books from City
    Lights,
Australian Aborigine song sticks, green temple incense, Tibetan
    precious-metal finger cymbals —
A broken leg a week later enough reminder, lay in bed and after few
    days' pain began to weep
no reason, thinking a little of Rabbi Schacter, a little of father Louis, a
    little
of everything that must be abandoned,
snow abandoned,
empty dog barks after the dogs have disappeared

meals eaten passed thru the body to nourish tomatoes and corn,
The wooden bowl from Haiti too huge for my salad,
Teachings, Tantras, Haggadahs, Zohar, Revelations, poetries, Koans
forgotten with the snowy world, forgotten
with generations of icicles crashing to white gullies by roadside,
Dharmakaya forgot, Nirmanakaya shoved in coffin, Sambhogakaya
    eclipsed in candle-light snuffed by the playful cat —
Goodbye my own treasures, bodies adored to the nipple,
old souls worshipped flower-eye or auditory panoramic awareness
    skull —
goodbye old socks washed over & over, blue boxer shorts, subzero
    longies,
new Ball Boots black hiplength for snowdrifts near the farm mailbox,
goodbye to my room full of books, all wisdoms I never studied, all the
    Campion, Creeley, Anacreon Blake I never read through,
blankets farewell, orange diamonded trunked from Mexico Himalayan
    sheepwool lugged down from Almora days with Lama
    Govinda and Peter trying to eat tough stubborn halfcooked chicken.
Paintings on wall, Maitreya, Sakyamuni & Padmasambhava,
    Dr. Samedi with Haitian spats & cane whiskey,
Bhaktivedanta Swami at desk staring sad eye Krishna at my hopeless
    selfconsciousness,
Attic full of toys, desk full of old checks, files on NY police & C.I.A.
    peddling Heroin,
Files on laughing Leary, files on Police State, files on ecosystems all
    faded & brown,
notebooks untranscribed, hundreds of little poems & prose my own
    hand,
newspaper interviews, assemblaged archives, useless paperworks sur-
    rounding me imperfectly chronologic, humorous later in eternity, re-
    flective of Cities' particular streets studios and boudoirs —
goodbye poetry books, I don't have to take you along anymore on a
    chain to Deux Magots like a red lobster
thru Paris, Moscow, Prague, Milan, New York, Calcutta, Bangkok, holy
    Benares, yea Rishikesh & Brindaban may yr prana lift ye over the
    roof of the world —
my own breath slower now, silent waiting & watching —
Downstairs pump-organs, musics, rags and blues, home made Blake
    hymns, mantras to raise the skull of America,
goodbye C chord, F chord, G chord, goodbye all the chords of The
    House of the Rising Sun
Goodbye farmhouse, city apartment, garbage subways Empire State,
    Museum of Modern Art where I wandered thru puberty dazzled by
    Van Gogh's raw-brained star-systems pasted on blue thick skyey
    Suchness —
Goodbye again Naomi, goodbye old painful legged poet Louis, goodbye
    Paterson the 69 between Joe Bozzo & Harry Haines that out-lasted
    childhood & poisoned the air o'er Passaic Valley,
goodbye Broadway, give my regards to the great falls & boys staring
    marijuana'd in wonder hearing the quiet roar of Godfather
    Williams' speech
Goodbye old poets of Century that taught fixed eye & sharp tongue
    from Pound with silent Mouni heart to Tom Veitch weeping in Stin-
    son Beach,
goodbye to my brothers who write poetry & play fiddle, my nephews
    who blow tuba & stroke bass viol, whistle flute or smile & sing in
    blue rhythm,
goodbye shades of dead living loves, bodies weeping bodies broken
    bodies aging, bodies turned to wax doll or cinder
Goodbye America you hope you prayer you tenderness, you IBM 135-

35 Electronic Automated Battlefield Igloo White Dragon-tooth Fuel-Air Bomb over Indochina
Goodbye Heaven, farewell Nirvana, sad Paradise adieu, adios all angels and archangels, devas & devakis, Bodhisattvas, Buddhas, rings of Seraphim, Constellations of elect souls weeping singing in the golden Bhumi Rungs, goodbye High Throne, High Central Place, Alleluiah Light beyond Light, a wave of the hand to Thee Central Golden Rose,
Om Ah Hum   A La La Ho Sophia, Soham Tara Ma, Om Phat Svaha Padmasambhava Marpa Mila sGam.po.pa Karmapa Trungpaye! Namastaji Brahma, Ave atque vale Eros, Jupiter, Zeus, Apollo, Surya, Indra
Bom Bom! Shivaye! Ram Nam Satyahey! Om Ganipatti, Om Saraswati Hrih Sowha! Ardinarishvara Radha Harekrishna faretheewell forevermore!
None left standing! No tears left for eyes, no eyes for weeping, no mouth for singing, no song for the hearer, no more words for any mind.

Cherry Valley, February 1, 1973

SPRING FASHIONS

Full moon over the shopping mall —
  in a display window's silent light
the naked mannequin observes her fingernails

Boulder, 1979

JUDY GRAHN

A WOMAN IS TALKING TO DEATH
(Part Three)

This woman is a lesbian be careful

In the military hospital where I worked
as a nurse's aide, the walls of the halls
were lined with howling women
waiting to deliver
or to have some parts removed.
One of the big private rooms contained
the general's wife, who needed
a wart taken off her nose.
we were instructed to give her special attention
not because of her wart or her nose
but because of her husband, the general.

as many women as men die, and that's a fact.

At work there was one friendly patient, already
claimed, a young woman burnt apart with X-ray,
she had long white tubes instead of openings;
rectum, bladder, vagina — I combed her hair, it
was my job, but she took care of me as if
nobody's touch could spoil her.

ho ho death, ho death
have you seen the twinkle in the dead woman's eye?

when you are a nurse's aide
someone suddenly notices you
and yells about the patient's bed,
and tears the sheets apart so you
can do it over, and over
while the patient waits
doubled over in her pain
for you to make the bed *again*
and no one ever looks at you,
only at what you do not do

Here, general, hold this soldier's bed pan
for a moment, hold it for a year —
then we'll promote you to making his bed.
we believe you wouldn't make such messes

if you had to clean up after them.

that's a fantasy.
this woman is a lesbian, be careful

When I was arrested and being thrown out
of the military, the order went out: dont anybody
speak to this woman, and for those three
long months, almost nobody did;   the dayroom, when
I entered it, fell silent til I had gone; they

were afraid, they knew the wind would blow
them over the rail, the cops would come,
the water would run into their lungs.
Everything I touched
was spoiled. They were my lovers, those
women, but nobody had taught us to swim.
I drowned, I took 3 or 4 others down
when I signed the confession of what we
had done   together.

No one will ever speak to me again.

I read this somewhere; I wasn't there:
in WW II the US army had invented some floating
amphibian tanks, and took them over to
the coast of Europe to unload them,
the landing ships all drawn up in a fleet,
and everybody watching. Each tank had a
crew of 6 and there were 25 tanks.
The first went down the landing planks
and sank, the second, the third, the
fourth, the fifth, the sixth went down
and sank. They weren't supposed
to sink, the engineers had
made a mistake. The crews looked around
wildly for the order to quit,
but none came, and in the sight of
thousands of men, each 6 crewmen
saluted his officers, battened down
his hatch in turn and drove into the
sea, and drowned, until all 25 tanks
were gone. did they have vacant
eyes, die laughing, or what? what
did they talk about, those men,
as the water came in?

was the general their lover?

Ah, Love, you smell of petroleum
and overwork
with grease on your fingernails,
paint in your hair
there is a pained look in your eye
from no appreciation
you speak to me of the lilacs
and appleblossoms we ought to have
the banquets we should be serving,
afterwards rubbing each other for hours
with tenderness and genuine
olive oil
someday. Meantime here is your cracked plate
with spaghetti. Wash your hands &
touch me, praise
my cooking. I shall praise your calluses.
we shall dance in the kitchen
of our imagination.

from THE COMMON WOMAN POEMS

Ella, in a Square Apron, Along Highway 80

She's a copperheaded waitress,
tired and sharp-worded, she hides
her bad brown tooth behind a wicked
smile, and flicks her ass
out of habit, to fend off the pass
that passes for affection.
She keeps her mind the way men
keep a knife — keen to strip the game
down to her size. She has a thin spine,
swallows her eggs cold, and tells lies.
She slaps a wet rag at the truck drivers
if they should complain. She understands
the necessity for pain, turns away
the smaller tips, out of pride, and
keeps a flask under the counter. Once,
she shot a lover who misused her child.
Before she got out of jail, the courts had pounced
and given the child away. Like some isolated lake,
her flat blue eyes take care of their own stark
bottoms. Her hands are nervous, curled, ready
to scrape.
The common woman is as common
as a rattlesnake.

Vera, From My Childhood

Solemnly swearing, to swear as an oath to you
who have somehow gotten to be a pale old woman;
swearing, as if an oath could be wrapped around
your shoulders
like a new coat:
For your 28 dollars a week and the bastard boss
you never let yourself hate;
and the work, all the work you did at home
where you never got paid;
For your mouth that got thinner and thinner
until it disappeared as if you had choked on it,
watching the hard liquor break your fine husband down
into a dead joke.
For the strange mole, like a third eye
right in the middle of your forehead;
for your religion which insisted that people
are beautiful golden birds and must be preserved;
for your persistent nerve
and plain white talk —
the common woman is as common
as good bread
as common as when you couldnt go on
but did.

For all the world we didnt know we held in common
all along
the common woman is as common as the best of bread
and will rise
and will become strong — I swear it to you
I swear it to you on my own head
I swear it to you on my common
woman's
head

Love rode 1500 miles on a grey
hound bus & climbed in my window
one night to surprise
both of us.
the pleasure of that sleepy
shock has lasted a decade
now or more because she is
always still doing it and I am
always still pleased. I do indeed like
aggressive women
who come half a continent
just for me; I am not saying that patience
is virtuous, Love
like anybody else, comes to those who
wait actively
and leave their windows open.

This is what is so odd
about your death:
that you will be 34 years old
the rest of my life.
We always said that we would be around
we two,
in our old age
& I still believe that,
however when I am 80
you will still be 34,
& how can we ever understand
what each other has been through?

I only have one reason for living
and that's you
And if I didn't have you as a
reason for living,
I would think of something else.

JACK GRAPES

I LIKE MY OWN POEMS

I like my own poems
best.
I quote from them
from time to time
saying, "A poet once said,"
and then follow up
with a line or two
from one of my *own* poems
appropriate to the event.
How those lines sing!
All that wisdom and beauty!
Why it tickles my ass
off its spine.
"Why those lines are mine!"
I say
and Jesus, what a bang
I get out of it.

I like the *ideas* in them,
my poems;
Ideas that hit home.
They *speak* to me.
I mean, I understand
what the hell
the damn poet's
talking about.
"Why I've been there,
the same thing," I shout,
and Christ! What a shot it is,
a shot.

And hey.
The words!
Whew!
I can hardly stand it.
Words sure do not fail
this guy, I say.
From some world
only he knows
he bangs the bong,
but I can feel it
in the wood,
in the wood of the word,
rising to its form
in the world.
"Now, you gotta be good
to do that!" I say
and damn! It just shakes
my heart,
you know!

PASSING THE KETCHUP

She says pass the ketchup
and I grab the salt shaker
and stretch it across the table.
"The ketchup," she says.

The lawn chair's full of rust
and the nylon straps in straggles.
It leans in the corner of the garage.
"Let's throw it out," she says.
"Not yet," I tell her. "Maybe we'll find
something to do with it."

We come home from the beach
and a trail of ants
flow to and from
the sugar bowl
down the counter to the floor
and out the screen door.
"Look at them all!" she shouts.
So I do.

These men grow old in my body.
They take such slow steps,
and take all morning
to drink a glass of milk.
They find nothing familiar
in the familiar,
debate the eye of the city
and the hand of the country.
They fall asleep in the kitchen.

"Where are the car keys?" she asks.
"The car keys," I repeat,
unable to remember
what is a car
and what is a key.
Finally:
"In the car," I say.
"The keys."

I wake in the middle of the night
to answer the phone.
Hello. Hello.
Nothing but the sound of someone's breathing
coming from the other end.
It sounds like my own,
but I can't be sure.
"Who was it?"
"Who was what?"
"On the phone!"
"Me. I think."

Today I sit on the beach
and watch the waves come in,
break in a stiff white line
forty feet out,
and carry the boogie-boarders
to the edge of the sand still standing.
There is nothing on the horizon.
Not a storm coming our way,
not a black ship,

no land.
We are all stretched on beach towels,
inching the white breast out for a tan.
We are all lying here at the edge
of a continent.

I get up and brush the sand from my body.
I take the napkins we brought
with the food in the ice-chest
and stick one each into my ears
and nose: wings of a sort.
Then another I roll for a fang.
Insert it under my top lip,
hunch over, and limp down the sand
like a walrus trying to dance
on the edge of the berm.
The kids step back at first,
then begin to mimic me;
finally, they join in, following me
as our footprints just above the water line
one on top of the other
change and grow larger, deeper.
A single new life form
come out of the water,
come out from the land.

"What do you think you're doing?" she calls.

"Passing the ketchup," I say.

HOME FREE

We're buying groceries for dinner
so I plunk two quarters into the slot machine
stationed by the check-out counter
and on the second quarter hit a $12 jackpot.
The tin cup is designed to make it seem like I've blown up
Fort Knox and bells go off to let the customers know
there's a silver waterfall, one to a customer.
I'm hooked and I know it.
I give the money away, three bucks apiece to Vern
and Katharine and Lori, saying here's some lucky quarters
but I'm really just trying not to hoard the luck,
too much might go off in my hands,
too much might alert the gods.
This luck is stolen, and after all the other luck
that's come my way — friends, talent, money — well,
I've got to be careful is all. Now we're in the casino,
the big time. Vern hits a $50 jackpot.
I'm at the blackjack table losing my breath.
Lori and Katharine are in the bar picking up strangers
while UCLA loses on a field goal to Arizona.
I lose another $20 at blackjack waiting for my free drink.
By the time we leave I'm $60 down, probably $100.
Next day at the Crystal Bay Club I pick up $100

at blackjack. Lori convinces me to leave a winner.
But I know I'll be back. The next morning we're back
and I drop $120. By the time we get to Reno
I can't tell for sure if I'm up or down.
Quarters go into the machines as I go by.
I'm pulling handles down the way I'd strip bark
from a tree or rickety-rick a stick against a fence
when I was a kid. I walk by a blackjack table, bet $40
and win. Walk off and put chips on roulette and lose.
Fork up a few bills at another table and win on two kings.
Bells go off, lights blink.
All you have to do here is win one jackpot,
one big fat fucking jackpot and the rest is history.
Lori's grabbing my arm and Katharine's hungry
and Vern's walking slow and easy out the door.
This quarter, this next quarter, this $5 yellow chip,
this $25 black chip, this is the one that does it,
one more plunk one more pull of the handle and it's done,
we're home free, we escape the pull of gravity,
we're off this rotten earth and heading for the stars.
"Lose here, win everywhere else," I say
as we get back in the car.
Merry Christmas, friends. Happy New Year.

JANA HARRIS

FIX ME A SALAMI SANDWICH HE SAID

Fix me a salami sandwich
he said
I don't wanna fix it myself
if you love me
you'll fix me a sandwich
you have to help me, he said
you have to take care of me
sometimes
he said
I need mothering
I need you to tell me
you love me
I need to hear you say it
I need you to sleep with me
I need you to fuck me
I need you to be on top
when we fuck
what time is it?
where's those phone numbers
that green matchbook with the raised
gold lettering
with the phone numbers
on the inside
I put it right here
I'm hungry
I haven't had time to get to the grocery
I need comforting
I need a ride to the corner
Let's have coffee together for once
he said
you make coffee
he said
I don't like these raw vegetables
I don't like this smelly cheese
it smells like cunt
he said
it smells like I have pussy
all over my fingers
you don't take care of me
he said
I have needs
he said
I have certain needs
and you don't do "Mommy"
very well, he said
you don't do "Mommy"
at all, he said.

DON'T CHEAPEN YOURSELF

You look sleazy tonight
ma said.
Cheap, I said
I'm doin cheap.
You got any idea
how much it costs
to do cheap these days?
To do City of Paris
three-inch platform sandals
and this I. Magnin snake dress?
I'm doin cheap.
You look like a bird, she said
a Halloween bird with red waxed lips.
   —In high school
you could either do cheap or Shakespeare,
college prep or a pointy bra,
ratting a bubble haircut
with a toilet brush.
I was not allowed to do high school cheap
I did blazers and wool skirts
from the Junior League thrift shop.
In high school it was
don't walk in the middle of
Richie, Leelee, and the baby,
you might come between them.
You look like a skag
wearin that black-eyed makeup,
people are gunna think you're cheap.
While I poured red food dye
on my hair
to match my filly's tail for the rodeo,
ma beat her head against the wall,
she said
tryin to make me nice.
I tried real hard,
but the loggers, the Navy guys,
they always hit on me.
Cause you're an easy mark, ma said.
And I played guilty,
I played guilty every time.
But now, I said
now I'm doing cheap.

PORTRAIT OF A GIRL AND
HER HORSE, 1965

I think of you often,
my sorrel Goldico horse.
You, who were the red
of the ribbed evening sky.
Hot summer days
belly-heavy in foal
we rode past the men
at the rock quarry
unafraid
rode through the aphrodisiac fields
of new mown hay
watching the flight of eagles
tormented by crows.
Behind the arch of your neck
I rode
to the rocks of the Clackamas River
worshiping
the bronzed power of your thighs.
Chariot horse
you swam the white water,
carried me sand-bar to sand-bar
til we were numb.
And those currents that drove us
across the mossed-granite rocks,
you knew them well
though they were silent
you knew them like the eels know them
knew them
like you knew the paths of the sun.
Goldico
those were summers with nights
too thick for sleeping
I drowned the dark spots of my soul
in that river
drifting downstream.
But now
though I know where you graze
with another foal
on some far hill near Oregon City
I cannot touch
what has gone.

DAVID KIRBY

MY FATHER IS ON THE PHONE

My father is on the phone,
saying, "I don't know what to say."
The rest of us are gathered around him,
frightened by sobs
coming out of the receiver
into which he says, "I don't know
what to say," over and over.
It seems there was a car,
and it crept through the orchard
with its lights out, and when
it stopped, there was a hole
in the roof, and the woman inside
was dead. In my grief
I think of Robinson Crusoe's collie
and my own hamster, never named,
sleeping beneath the earth,
as my father stares at the phone,
saying the same thing over
and over again, saying
"I don't know what to say."

TO MY SONS

Boys, forgive me: if I'm ill-tempered in the morning,
it's because I spend my nights saving you from men
far worse than the monsters in your books.
You wouldn't believe these jaspers.
Why, once they took you to Mexico
and kept you awake for a week
and made you sit in straightback chairs
in a room where rattlesnakes slithered on the floor.
You fellows should have seen your dad:
just as you were falling off the chairs,
I kicked the door in and scooped you up.
With a boy under each arm, I stamped the snakes
to death and laid out the guards with spin kicks
to the groin and temple. We ran like hell
for the jeep and the survivors opened fire,
but we got out of there thanks to some fancy wheel work,
and now that we're home again with your mother,
I just want to say that I hope you boys
were paying attention back there in Mexico,
because you might be fathers yourselves some day
and believe me, those men will still be there.

SALAD FOR BREAKFAST

This morning half of me
watches you sleep,
your arm over your head,
while the other half
writes the screenplay
for one of the best movies
ever made. In it
two lovers are walking
through the streets of Paris at dawn.
They are on their way to Sacré Coeur,
where the priests are waiting
to marry them. The lovers are us.
The ceremony is quiet and simple,
but afterwards there is a big party.
The priests make an enormous salad
and dress it with oil
and egg yolk and lemon juice.
There is enough for the whole city.
Soon everyone is dancing
and eating salad by the plateful.
They do not know it,
but you have the most beautiful breasts
in the world.
Suddenly there is a commotion:
a bearded man has been caught
with a vial of poison.
He is dunked in the river three times
and sent into exile.
I put my hand on your stomach.
"All of Paris is happy," I say.
Eyes still closed, you smile
and lick your lips.

TO A FRENCH STRUCTURALIST

There's no modesty, Todorov,
in the park where I read:
the young mothers and working girls
raise their skirts and open their blouses
to the sun while the children play,
the old men doze, and I wrestle
with your *Poetics*. When I look again,
perhaps they'll all be naked;
they'll make for the seesaw and jungle gym,
bosoms swinging and long legs flashing
in the midday light. Ah, that clerk
at the Préfecture de Police
looked at me with such disdain
when he asked what I was doing in Paris!
It was a lie, Todorov,
when I shrugged and said, "Nothing."

RON KOERTGE

GERRY AND I

were taken by Tucson, not by the graduate school —
it was a cruddy little fiefdom — but by Tucson,
palmy and unfurled, and by Tucson's spell-binding
nights which lured some people to screw in the
ocotillo, others like my landlord to squat
in the underbrush looking for UFO's, Gerry and me
to drink from sundown til 2:00, then buy a six pack
and settle on my front porch — a peninsula
of good sense and comity — to contemplate
the green grass at our feet.

Across the fence, across the road, beyond the campus
deep in cyclopedic sleep lay the men who taught
or taught with us, already bound to their wives
like Ulysses to the mast or at 23 dead at the center
or both.

We were afraid it would happen to us but did not dwell
on that. The liquor made us vatic and goofy and polite;
regularly we slipped off the porch and took a few
discreet steps into the moonlight.

I didn't notice it was killing the grass until
my landlord cornered me — "You never heard the sound
or saw the light? This is an electro-galactic fission
burn if I ever saw one." Pretty soon some Air Force
brass showed up and sighted, measured, recorded,
dug, bottled, felt, smelled, tasted
the big brown spot which grew as exams marshalled,
as the women I loved fled to better footing,
as Gerry's wife went East. For a visit.

The sassy, rudderless nights were numbered
but we sat while we could and, when we stood,
worked our way toward the street.
"You'll have to leave," said my landlord. "Outer
Space Ltd. is sealing off the area."

I got my few things together. He walked me to the
car. "You know," he said, "I've seen them. Not the craft
but I've seen the aliens. One large. One small. They
must need constant nourishment as they're never without
their food supply; they come out of the shadows
separately, stand there for a few moments staring
at our world, then retreat."

I looked back at the porch, my eyes vaulting the pale
grass. Christ, it had been fine.

"You know," he said putting his hand on my shoulder.
"You're lucky to be alive."

LILITH

She did not graze on all fours but
wrapped her arms and legs around Adam
and said, "Oh, Daddy. It feels so good,"
and he promised her a little place of
her own in Manhattan.

God saw that he had made a mistake
and put him to sleep, wiped his brain
smooth as a grape and tried again with
Eve

who lay flat on her back, arms and
legs extended as if she had fallen from
a tree. As Adam tried, she talked out
loud, "So much to do, so many animals
to name, so much adoration to give
Him."

Adam rolled off her, sat up holding his
side. "It hurts," he said.
"What does?"
"Here."
"That's called a rib."
"No. Above that."
"Your heart. I've only been here ten
minutes and already I know ever so much
more than you."
"I think it's broken."
"Oh, pooh. Everything's wonderful and
all you do is complain. You should be
glad you're not an insurance salesman."

Adam had to admit she was right, yet
what was that smell of crushed fern,
such heat disguised as words, a vision:
lovely toes pointing toward the sun.

"Sorrow," he said, "I feel sorrow."
"You eat too fast," said Eve. "It's gas."

LAZARUS

After Jesus raised him from the dead and everybody was impressed,
He went on His way while Lazarus stayed home with Mary and
Martha. At first they were glad to have him back, but
time took care of that.

"Don't shake hands with him," said one guest, "he's
colder than a well-digger's ass."
"Lazarus is pale as hell," said an uncle.
A niece added, "Lazarus stinks."

Pretty soon they had him sitting nine yards away from the table,
wrapped in a blanket, discreetly downwind.

Finally he moved back to the tomb, going out only in the
evening to follow the sun into the West,

God's name in vain on his cracked and loamy lips.

ORIENTATION WEEK

and a family of two is exploring the Student Union.
Dad is all decked out in the shirt she bought with
her own money. Joyce is wearing snug cut-offs and
her freshman breasts stir as she walks.

Dad knows that all the boys plan to slip some LSD
in her cocoa as soon as he is out of sight. He
takes in the monsters, their hair down to there,
a fuselage in every pair of pants.

Worse than he expected, certainly not the eunuchs
and mild wethers that he hoped for. And where is
The Jake Barnes Dormitory?

He sees them do it to her even as they stand by the
car. Worse, he sees her ask for it, coaxing with
her expensive teeth. Why can't he

Lock those vivid hips in her room?
Follow her everywhere, revolvers drawn?
Punch a few of those furry bastards in the chops?

So he does what he can — lips to chaste brow, hand
to bare arm saying,

Goodby, now. Be good.

THE LITTLE DUTCH BOY

Don's wife Linda wants to go to bed
with a plumber named
Rex.

Don has laid down
the law: if she is ever unfaithful
to him, he will divorce her and take
the children.

"God, what should I do?" says Linda,
handles coming off, porcelain collapsing,

water everywhere.

I'D BE AFRAID THAT I'D DROP A BABY

she said.

We'd been talking about a nurse we knew who
threw them around like dolls.

I'm just sure I'd drop it, she repeated
falling against her husband's side in a
kind of swoon.

Midnight, he said. Past somebody's bedtime.

THE CONVERSION

Each Sunday morning we put on our good clothes
and, to save wear and tear on the car,
walked to church three abreast. I was dressed
like a miniature Dad; I courted
my giant wife.

On our way, we passed the Boling's big ranch
style home. Alan was outside shooting baskets
and I waved. My parents' eyes were fixed.
Only I saw the mother carelessly
wrapped as a last minute gift.

My mother especially disapproved of the Bolings
and though I knew Alan was black as anthracite
inside I liked him. We rode our Schwinn
bikes together and shot B-B guns
with Red Ryder's name on the stock.

Once I saw Mrs. Boling having a drink
in still another careless gown. "See her
nips?" asked Alan. "She walks around like that
all the time. I think she wants me to
fuck her."

I was sure he would be dead by morning, smothered
in the arctic arms of the Holy Ghost,
but if he happened to be spared in order to die
later, at 18 perhaps, writhing on Skid Row
with cancer of the penis, I knew it was my duty
to see if he might not yet be saved.

Bible Camp was not far away, and I invited him.
He was attractive and would find a girlfriend,
too, one who would also French kiss
and then wonder if her tongue would dry up
like a weed.

Alan wanted to know what else we could do:
"Lots of things. Take walks."
"Hike?"
I thought of the short paths that led to
the highway. "Sort of."
"Can we ride or shoot?"
"Shoot what?"
"Game. Skeet."
"No, but there's always the recreation period."
"With polo?"
I thought of the ping pong table and its
lost ball. "Well . . ."
"Movies then. Comedies?"
"There's movies all the time. They aren't
too funny but sometimes you can see the nips
on the lady heathens."
When the lepers
weren't in the way.

I went alone. My girl friend was sporting
large breasts. We watched the doomed natives,
we listened to the preachers thin and fierce
as hounds. At night I dreamed of Alan Boling
perched on an English saddle alternately
watching Martin & Lewis and bringing down

game birds with a golden gun.

Joyce knew I was troubled and showed me
her new bra saying it was all right
if we did not go any farther until
after the ceremony.

I lay among the marshalled trees,
the sky cupped over me like a hand.
As surely as I had known what a sinner
I was I knew that I was a boy with few prospects,
that I had no idea what the world was like
but the King James version, that I was dumber
than any benighted native, that if I was not careful
I would marry this girl and tithe and die.

My parents did not understand what happened
at Bible Camp. They did not understand
why I no longer went to church. They did not
understand why I despised everything they
had taught me or why I feared a life like theirs,
as narrow as a bottle's neck.

My mother cried all the time and looked
for reasons. "Is it that Boling boy?"
she asked. "Is he responsible? Was it him?"

I shrugged inside my leather jacket. I went
outside and smoked, listening to her pray and wail,
unwilling then to answer any question about any-
thing and even now half unwilling but able
anyway to say, if it's still so important,

"Yes, Mother. It was him."

MY WIFE

is outside calling the cat. She
is barefoot and the wind under her
dress holds it high on her thighs.

Grief has softened her pleas to a
single cry. I hear her advance and
retreat on the dark boulevard. She
has one hand to her lips, echo-style.

Now the neighbors will think that
she is near mad from malignancy
or that our life together is empty
as a cave.

The truth is that she admires the cat
who eats here. He has balls like
ornaments and is fierce in
his affections.

WHAT SHE WANTED

was my bones. As I gave them
to her one at a time she put
them in a bag from Saks.

As long as I didn't hesitate
she collected scapula and
vertebrae with a smile.

If I grew reluctant she pouted.
Then I would come across with
rib cage or pelvis.

Eventually I lay in a puddle
at her feet, only the boneless
penis waving like an anemone.

"Look at yourself," she said.
"You're disgusting."

FOR MY DAUGHTER

She often lies with her hands behind her head
in a San Quentin pose, arms forming a pair
of small empty wings.

She does not slip from the bath in a loose
towel, affording Follies' glimpses
of rump and thigh. She does lumber by
in a robe of immense dunciness.

Her dates are fixed up or blind
often, like specimens, behind thick glass.
She leaves late, returns by 12:00 afraid
perhaps that she will turn into
something worse.

She comes to me and wants to know what to do.
I say I do not know.
She comes to me and wants to know if it will
ever be all right.
I say Yes but it will take a long time.

STEVE KOWIT

HELL

I died & went to Hell & it was nothing like L.A.
The air all shimmering & blue. No windows
busted, gutted walk-ups, muggings, rapes.
No drooling hoodlums hulking in the doorways.
Hell isn't anything like Ethiopia or Bangladesh or Bogota:
beggars are unheard of. No one's starving. Nobody
lies moaning in the streets. Nor is it Dachau
with its ovens, Troy in flames, some slaughterhouse
where squealing animals, hung upside down, are bled & skinned.
No plague-infested Avignon or post-annihilation Hiroshima.
Quite the contrary: in Hell everybody's health is fine
forever, & the weather is superb — eternal spring.
The countryside all wildflowers & the cities
hum with commerce: cargo ships bring all the latest
in appliances, home entertainment, foreign culture, silks.
Folks fall in love, have children. There is sex
& romance for the asking. In a word, the place is perfect.
Only, unlike Heaven, where when it rains
the people are content to let it rain,
in Hell they live like we do — endlessly complaining.
Nothing as it is is ever right. The astroturf
a nuisance, neighbors' kids too noisy, traffic
nothing but a headache. If the patio were just
a little larger, or the sunroof on the Winnebago worked.
If only we had darker eyes or softer skin or longer legs,
lived elsewhere, plied a different trade, were slender,
sexy, wealthy, younger, famous, loved, athletic.
Friend, I swear to you as one who has returned
if only to bear witness: no satanic furies
beat their kited wings. No bats shriek overhead.
There are no flames. No vats of boiling oil
wait to greet us in that doleful kingdom.
Nothing of the sort. The gentleman who'll ferry you across
is all solicitude & courtesy. The river black but calm.
The crossing less eventful than one might have guessed.
Though no doubt you will think it's far too windy on the water.
That the glare is awful. That you're tired, hungry, ill
at ease, or that, if nothing else, the quiet is unnerving.
That you need a drink, a cigarette, a cup of coffee.

LURID CONFESSIONS

One fine morning they move in for the pinch
& snap on the cuffs — just like that.
Turns out they've known all about you for years,
have a file the length of a paddy-wagon
with everything — tapes, prints, film . . .
the whole shmear. Don't ask me how but
they've managed to plug a mike into one of your molars
& know every felonious move & transgression
back to the very beginning, with ektachromes
of your least indiscretion & peccadillo.
Needless to say, you are thrilled,
tho sitting there in the docket
you bogart it, tough as an old tooth —
your jaw set, your sleeves rolled
& three days of stubble . . . Only,
when they play it back it looks different:
a life common & loathsome as gum stuck to a chair.
Tedious hours of you picking your nose,
scratching, eating, clipping your toenails . . .
Alone, you look stupid; in public, your rapier
wit is slimy & limp as an old bandaid.
They have thousands of pictures of people around you
stifling yawns. As for sex — a bit
of pathetic groping among the unlovely & luckless:
a dance with everyone making steamy love in the dark
& you alone in a corner eating a pretzel.
You leap to your feet protesting
that's not how it was, they have it all wrong.
But nobody hears you. The bailiff
is snoring, the judge is cleaning his teeth,
the jurors are all wearing glasses with eyes painted open.
The flies have folded their wings & stopped buzzing.
In the end, after huge doses of coffee,
the jury is polled. One after another
they manage to rise to their feet
like narcoleptics in August, sealing your fate:
Innocent . . . innocent . . . innocent . . . Right down the line.
You are carried out screaming.

THEY ARE LOOKING FOR CHE GUEVARA

The lecturer writes the phrase *free enterprise* on the board in green
    chalk.
Above it white pustular fissures appear, which is the strangler
fig taking root in that part of the map devoted to Indonesia.
The metallic pit of the fruit grown from the miracle seed of the green
    revolution begins ticking.
The peasants dig in. The secret bombing begins.
The porpoise & bison & whooping crane lie down on top of the
    lecturer's desk & begin disappearing.
Meanwhile the Huns push on to the Yalu River
searching for Che Guevara.
The CIA is hunting for him in the Bolivian Andes.

Ferdinand Marcos & 6,000 Green Berets are hunting for him in the
    Philippines.
Ian Smith is hunting him down in Zimbabwe.
A small flame appears in the map of Asia:
it is that part they have burnt down searching for Che Guevara,
    queen-bee of the revolution.
They are hunting for him in Angola, Korea, Guatemala, the Congo,
    Brazil, Iran, Greece, Lebanon, Chile.
9,000 Ozymandian paratroops drop over Santo Domingo with
    searchlights, searching for him.
He is not there. He is gone. He is hiding among the Seminoles.
He throws the knife into the treaty with Osceola.
He conspires with Denmark Vesey.
In Port-au-Prince he is with Toussaint.
He reappears later at Harper's Ferry.
He is in Nicaragua, in Cuba where they have embargoed the rain.
The CIA has traced him to Berkeley, but he is in Algeria too
& Uruguay, Spain, Portugal, Guam, Puerto Rico.
Not all the ears of the dead of Asia will lead them to him.
He goes home, embraces his wife, embraces Hildita, embraces the
    children of Buenos Aires,
gives his compadre Fidel an *abrazo*,
pours a cup of *maté*, takes a pill for his asthma,
cleans his rifle, reloads it, writes the First Declaration of Havana.
Torpedoes of Intergalactic Capital Inc. blow up the screaming hair of
    the global village.
B52s drone overhead. It is dawn. They are checking every frontier.
    They are looking for Che Guevara.

NOTICE

This evening, the sturdy Levis
I wore every day for over a year
& which seemed to the end in perfect condition,
suddenly tore.
How or why I don't know,
but there it was— a big rip at the crotch.
A month ago my friend Nick
walked off a racquetball court,
showered,
got into his street clothes,
& halfway home collapsed & died.
Take heed you who read this
& drop to your knees now & again
like the poet Christopher Smart
& kiss the earth & be joyful
& make much of your time
& be kindly to everyone,
even to those who do not deserve it.
For although you may not believe it will happen,
you too will one day be gone.
I, whose Levis ripped at the crotch
for no reason,
assure you that such is the case.
Pass it on.

JOANNE KYGER

DESTRUCTION

First of all do you remember the way a bear goes through
a cabin when nobody is home? He goes through
the front door. I mean he really goes *through* it. Then
he takes the cupboard off the wall and eats a can of lard.

He eats all the apples, limes, dates, bottled decaffeinated
coffee, and 35 pounds of granola. The asparagus soup cans
fall to the floor. Yum! He chomps up Norwegian crackers
stashed for the winter. And the bouillon, salt, pepper,
paprika, garlic, onions, potatoes.

                He rips the Green Tara
poster from the wall. Tries the Coleman Mustard. Spills
the ink, tracks in the flour. Goes up stairs and takes
a shit. Rips open the water bed, eats the incense and
drinks the perfume. Knocks over the Japanese tansu
and the Persian miniature of a man on horseback watching
a woman bathing.

            Knocks *Shelter, Whole Earth Catalogue,*
Planet Drum, Northern Mists, Truck Tracks, and
Women's Sports into the oozing water bed mess.

                    He goes
down stairs and out the back wall. He keeps on going
for a long way and finds a good cave to sleep it all off.
Luckily he ate the whole medicine cabinet, including stash
of LSD, Peyote, Psilocybin, Amanita, Benzedrine, Valium
and aspirin.

"OF ALL THINGS FOR YOU TO GO AWAY MAD"

Of all things for you to go away mad on a tender morning like this
although grey for the 8th day in sunny california
because I asked you to change your shirt after the third day
because the neckline won't come clean
and you said you preferred dirty necklines
and I hurled the pancake turner on the floor
shouting what about appearances
and you said it took a long time to see through appearances
   and what do we care
     and you got no breakfast, no pancake, forget it. I hope
      you eat some lunch.
        And at 12:30 you still got no lunch which information
via the phone I find out because I want to tell you I am sorry

about the pancakes and appearances, grey day, the Pride of Madeira
fallen over in the garden. Plucked and plumed, all show, no heart,
heavy headed, no answer, breathe deeply.
                              Enough of slumber land. I've put
                              beans on for dinner.
We'll sit at the table, and don't put me on, the room in my heart
gets nourished, by your friendly handsome looks. You read
a lot of books.

AND WITH MARCH A DECADE IN BOLINAS

Just sitting around smoking, drinking and telling stories,
the news, making plans, analyzing, approaching the cessation
of personality, the single personality understands its demise.
Experience of the simultaneity of all human beings on this planet,
alive when you are alive. This seemingly inexhaustible
sophistication of awareness becomes relentless and horrible,
trapped. How am I ever going to learn enough to get out.

The beautiful soft and lingering props of the Pacific here.

                    The back door bangs
          So we've made a place to live
          here in the greened out 70's
                         Trying to talk in the tremulous
                morality of the present
          Great Breath, I give you, Great Breath!

January 23, 1979

DORIANNE LAUX

THE LAUNDROMAT

My clothes somersault in the dryer. At thirty
I float in and out of a new kind of horniness,
the kind where you get off on words and gestures,
long talks about Art are foreplay, the climax
is watching a man eat a napoleon while he drives.
Across from me a fifty year old matron
folds clothes, her eyes focused on the nipples
of a young man in silk jogging shorts. He looks up,
catching her. She giggles and blurts out, "Hot, isn't it?"
A man on my right eyes the line of my shorts, waiting
for me to bend over. I do. An act of animal kindness.
A long black jogger swings in off the street
to splash his face in the sink and I watch the room
become a sweet humid jungle. We crowd around the Amazon
at the watering hole twitching our noses like wildebeests
or buffalo, snorting, rooting out mates in the heat.
I want to hump every moving thing in this place.
I want to lie down in the dry dung and the dust
and twist to scratch my back.
I want to stretch and prowl and grow lazy in the shade.
I want to have a slew of cubs.
"Do you have change for a quarter?" he says,
scratching the inside of his thigh.
Back in the laundromat my socks are sticking
to my sheets. Caught in the crackle of static electricity
I fold my underwear. Noticing the honey colored stains
in each silk crotch, odd-shaped, like dreams, I make
the panties into neat squares and drop them, smiling,
into the wicker basket.

GHOSTS

It's midnight and a light rain falls.
I sit on the front stoop to smoke.
Across the street a lit window, filled
with a ladder on which a young man stands.
His head dips into the frame each time
he sinks his brush in the paint.

He's painting his kitchen white, patiently
covering the faded yellow with long strokes.
He leans into his work like a lover, risks
losing his balance, returns gracefully
to the precise middle of the step

to dip and start again.

A woman appears beneath his feet, borrows
paint, takes it onto her thin brush
like a tongue. Her sweater is the color
of tender lemons. This is the beginning
of their love, bare and simple
as that wet room.

My hip aches against the damp cement.
I take it inside, punch up a pillow
for it to nest in. I'm getting too old
to sit on the porch in the rain,
to stay up all night, watch morning
rise over rooftops.
              Too old to dance
circles in dirty bars, a man's hands
laced at the small of my spine, pink
slingbacks hung from limp fingers. Love.
I'm too old for that. The foreign tongues
loose in my mouth, teeth that rang
my breasts by the nipples like soft bells.

I want it back. The red earrings and blue
slips. Lips alive with spit. Muscles
twisting like boat ropes in a hard wind.
Bellies for pillows. Not this ache in my hip.

I want the girl who cut through blue poolrooms
of smoke and golden beers, stepping out alone
into a summer fog to stand beneath a street lamp's
amber halo, her blue palms cupped
around the flare of a match.

She could have had so many lives. Gone off
with a boy to Arizona, lived on a ranch
under waves of carved rock, her hands turned
the color of flat red sands. Could have said
yes to a woman with fingers tapered as candles,
or a man who slept in a canvas tepee, who pulled
her down on his mattress of grass where she made
herself as empty as the gutted fire.
                 Oklahoma.
I could be there now, spinning corn from dry
cobs, working fat tomatoes into mason jars.

The rain has stopped. For blocks the houses
drip like ticking clocks. I turn off lights
and feel my way to the bedroom, slip cold
toes between flowered sheets, nest my chest
into the back of a man who sleeps in fits,
his suits hung stiff in the closet, his racked
shoes tipped toward the ceiling.

This man loves me for my wit, my nerve,
for the way my long legs fall from hemmed skirts.
When he rolls his body against mine I know
he feels someone else. There's no blame.
I love him, even as I remember a man with cane-
brown hands, palms pink as blossoms opening
over my breasts.
           He holds me,
even with all those other fingers wrestling
inside me, even with all those other shoulders
wedged above his own like wings.

QUARTER TO SIX

                              and the house swept
with the colors of dusk, I set the table
with plates and lace. In these minutes
left to myself, before the man and child
scuff at the doorstep and come in,
I think of you and wonder what I would say
if I could write. Would I tell you
how I avoid his eyes, this man
I've learned to live with, afraid of what
he doesn't know about me. That I've finished
a pack of cigarettes in one sitting, to ready myself
for dinner, where my hands will waver over a plate
of fish as the bones of my daughter grow normal
in the chair beside me. Missy

                         this is what's become of the wedding
you swore you'd come to wearing black. That was in 1970
as we sat on the bleached floor of the sanitarium
sharing a cigarette you'd won in a game of pool.
You said even school was better than this ward
where they placed the old men in their draped pants,
or the housewives screaming in loud flowered shifts
as they clung to the doors that lined the halls.
When we ate our dinner of fish and boiled potatoes
it was you who nudged me under the table
when the thin man in striped pajamas climbed the chair
beside me in his bare feet, his pink-
tinged urine making soup of my leftovers. With my eyes
locked on yours I watched you keep eating. So I lifted
my fork to my open mouth, jello quivering green
against the tines, and while I trusted you and chewed
on nothing, he leapt into the arms of the night nurse
and bit open the side of her face. You had been there

                         longer, knew the ropes, how to take
the sugar-coated pill and slip it into the side pocket
of your mouth, pretend to swallow it down in drowsy
gulps while the white-frocked nurse eyed the clockface
above our heads. You tapped messages into the wall
while I wept and struggled to remember the code, snuck in
after bedcount with cigarettes, blew the blue smoke
through barred windows. We traded stories, our military
fathers, yours locking you in the closet for the days
it took to chew ribbons of flesh from your fingers,
your dresses piled into a bed — mine, who worked
his ringed fingers inside me while the house
slept, my face pressed to the pillow, my fists
knotted into the sheets. Some nights

                         I can't eat. The dining room fills
with their chatter, my hand stuffed with the glint
of a fork and the safety of butter knives
quiet at the sides of our plates. If I could write you now
I'd tell you I wonder how long I can go on with this careful
pouring of the wine from its bottle, straining to catch it
in the fragile glass.

                         Tearing open my bread
I see the scar, stitches laced up the root
of your arm, the flesh messy where you grabbed at it
with the broken glass of an ashtray. That was

the third time. And later you laughed
when they twisted you into the white strapped jacket
demanding you vomit the pills. I imagined you
in the harsh light of a bare bulb where you took
the needle without flinching, retched
when the ipecac hit you, your body shelved over
the toilet and no one to hold the hair
from your face. I don't know

        where your hands are now, the fingers
that filled my mouth those nights you tongued me open
in the broken light that fell through chicken-wired windows.
The intern found us and wrenched us apart, the half-moon
of your breast exposed as you spit on him.
"Now you're going to get it." he hissed
through his teeth and you screamed "Get what?"
as if there was anything anyone could give you.
If I could write you now I'd tell you

        I still see your face, bone white
as my china above the black velvet cape you wore
to my wedding twelve years ago, the hem
of your black crepe skirt brushing up the dirty rice
in swirls as you swept down the reception line
to kiss me. "Now you're going to get it." you whispered,
cupping my cheek in your hand.

THE CATCH

The film footage wavers
on the grey TV screen, a fist
full of Marines flung
from a helicopter, a flower
suspended in air
dropping a bloom of pods.
A row of khakied backs, the square-
shouldered shapes of men, knee-deep
in mud and raising rifles
like fishing rods.
There is the bitter smell of powder,
of too much salt, as bodies
are scooped from a trench and flopped
like fish on a deck.
Here's what is left
of a boy from Maryland, half a face
and his good right arm. The rest,
scattered on a hillside, his pink
testicles split against
the brain-grey rock. In his breast
pocket, a snapshot, his girl
in a bikini, her whole body sprawled
across the hood of a new Camaro.
She's wet from the blue pool, shining,
car keys dangling from her teeth like minnows.

TEACHING POETRY WITH PICTURES ← political

Small for a fifth grader, hand raised,
he wants to know if his poem is finished,
is it good, is it right.
I'm too tired to give the lecture again:
Poetry is yours. There is no right.
It's finished if you want it to be finished.

Kneeling next to Thong Phan
I look at the picture he's chosen:
a lone American Indian
folded into a spindle chair.
The shack above his shoulders slumps,
swaybacked, a wasted prairie beyond.

I ask him to read what he's written.
In chopped English he quietly recites:

> This man is older and he sit
> and he do nothing and I don't
> know what he look into and house
> look like house in Vietnam.
> He think about the animal
> and his face look like sad
> and he wait hard for all his family
> to come home.

I reach for the poem and touch
his small-boned hand. The past
pushes through me. The pictures.
One framed in my livingroom TV:
a girl with no hands in his country
holds what's left of her mother
in her arms.

Has his mother told him about us?
Or are her own nightmares enough?
Or doesn't she know the words
in any language that can explain
how he learns poetry
from the sister of a boy
who tossed a match to a village,
watched it crumble to kindling.

A girl whose sweetheart sent home
snapshots of himself, crewtopped
in Marine greens, slouched
in the doorway of a hootch
with his buddies, making crazy faces.

I want to tell him that I wrote letters
less often each week, dreamed of fire
eating the streets, that when I opened
a magazine to naked women in a ditch
I wanted him to die, that when he came home
and stood in my doorway whole, I began
to hate what seemed indestructible.

My face buried in his shoulder I let him
hold me while he cried, my arms pinned
hard to my sides, his gold buttons
digging into my chest. But that night
in my back yard I tore his letters
to shreds, the pale blue paper falling

into the mouth of the garbage can.

I want to tell Thong Phan the truth,
that my brother still wakes gagging
into clutched pillows, that our mother
drags his mattress to the patio to dry,
brown stains set in the pin-striped ticking
like the outlines of maps.
But I'd have to tell all of it:
that he calls us gooks over breakfast,
stabs his fork into eggs and ham,
the pink flesh parting beneath his knife.

And Thong Phan fidgets in my silence, waits
for me to tell him what to do, his hair
swirling toward me like blackened thatching.
I smooth it with my open palm, give him
back his poem and say, "Yes, it is good.
It is right. It is finished."

CHINA

From behind he looks like a man
I once loved, that hangdog slouch
to his jeans, a sweater vest, his neck
thick veined as a horse cock, a halo
of chopped curls.

He orders coffee and searches
his pockets, first in front, then
from behind, a long finger sliding
into the slitted denim like that man
slipped his thumb into me one summer
as we lay after love, our freckled
bodies two plump starfish on the sheets.

Semen leaked and pooled in his palm
as he moved his thumb slowly,
not to excite me, just to affirm
he'd been there.

I have loved other men since, taken
them into my mouth like a warm vowel,
lain beneath them and watched their irises
float like small worlds in their open eyes.

But this man pressed his thumb
toward the tail of my spine
like he was entering
China, or a ripe papaya
so that now when I think of love,
I think of this.

NAOMI LAZARD

MISSING FATHER REPORT

Your help is urgently needed.
If you have any information
regarding the whereabouts
of the following individual
contact us immediately.

Subject is, or was, about 45
at the time of disappearance.
Last seen dissolving slowly,
first the back of his neck
then his shoulders went away,
his legs left too. In the end
his face vanished without warning,
the mouth open, still speaking.

We have no indication why
this person, of all people,
should have disappeared.
Reliable witnesses have stated
that not even his eyes endured,
not even the tips of his fingers.

You will know him by certain signs,
by the innocent look of his hair
falling over his forehead
in moments of emotional upheaval,
by his hands which are fine
and arrive like delicate instruments
of mercy.

        You will also know him
by his eyes which have an unblinking
quality like those of a horse
or some other friendly, domesticated
animal. You will know him
if you are prepared.

There is no history of mental disease,
no police file. Disappearance was,
for all practical purposes,
voluntary. Subject's last
formal statement, for the record,
was "I love you,"
or something like that.

THE WIND

When the wind howls at the window
with your mother's voice,
when she knocks there with her shoe —
don't leave her out in the cold.
Though you never said anything
she was glad to hear, though
you stopped trying to please her
before you started school, let her in.
It is your life she is battering
with her sad muddy shoe on the panes.
As if you truly need her, as if you mean it,
make room for her in the bed beside you.
She won't open her eyes.
When you take her in your arms
she will fall apart like ashes.
Best not to touch her;
make a hollow in your pillow
for her dust to settle in.
It will be just a spoonful,
enough to stir into your coffee
when you wake up in the morning.

ORDINANCE ON ARRIVAL

Welcome to you
who have managed to get here.
It's been a terrible trip;
you should be happy you have survived it.
Statistics prove that not many do.
You would like a bath, a hot meal,
a good night's sleep. Some of you
need medical attention.
None of this is available.
These things have always been
in short supply; now
they are impossible to obtain.

                This is not
a temporary situation;
it is permanent.
Our condolences on your disappointment.
It is not our responsibility
everything you have heard about this place
is false. It is not our fault
you have been deceived,
ruined your health getting here.
For reasons beyond our control
there is no vehicle out.

ORDINANCE ON WINNING

Congratulations.
The suspense is over. You are the winner.
The doubts you have had
concerning the rules of the contest,
about the ability and fairness of the judges,
were illfounded. The rumors
pertaining to a "fix"
have been exposed as nonsense.
The contest is fair and always has been.
Now that the results are in
your prize will be sent to you
under separate cover. Be sure to have
your social security number
or other proper identification
for the postman.
                    Upon receiving it
contact us immediately
in order that you may be notified
of further developments, ensuing publicity,
other honors which will be forthcoming.
If by some chance your prize does not arrive
as scheduled, do not bother to inform us.

Our responsibility is discharged
with this announcement.
In the event that you do not receive
your prize, there is no authority
to whom you can turn
for information or redress.
We advise you to wait patiently
for your prize
which will either come or not.

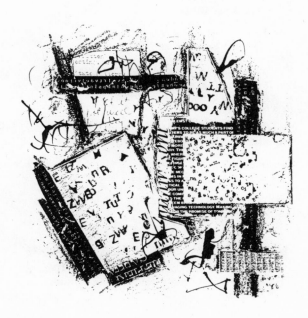

GERALD LOCKLIN

ON THE RACK

i know she is hypersensitive
about her athletic stature,
her pretty smile,
her general wholesomeness,
which everyone except her considers attractive,

so i never miss a chance to allude to
farmers' daughters, sturdiness,
good breeders, and germanic stock;

and since i know she is insanely jealous,
i seldom let an evening go by
without a mention of some beautiful
and temporarily available woman
that i've run into earlier in the day;

and because she's needlessly self-conscious
about her weight,
i wouldn't think of letting a day go by
without suggesting that i run out for
a matterhorn pizza
lest she collapse within the hour
of malnutrition.

if she were a puritan,
i'd ridicule her for that,
but since she loves sex
and has few inhibitions,
i do my best to make her feel
like a nymphomaniac.

these are the ways in which i keep her
anxious, humble, and dependent.
these are the ways
in which i punish her.

and what was her offense:

that she restored my confidence
when i was nearly broken
on the rack.

RIVERRUN PAST DICK AND JANE

There are those who consider Finnegans Wake obscure,
but they have not taught Freshman Composition.

POOP

my daughter, blake, is in kindergarten. they are teaching her to be a
docile citizen and, incidentally to read. concurrently, like many of
us, she has become a trifle anal compulsive. complications ensue.

i ask her what she has learned today. she says, "i learned the pledge
of allegiance." "how does it go?" i ask. "it goes," she says, "i poop
allegiance to the poop of the united poops of ameripoop."

"that's good," i say, "that's very good. what else?" "o say can you
poop, by the dawn's early poop, what so proudly we pooped . . ."

for christmas, she improvises, "away in a pooper, all covered with
poop, the little lord poopus lay pooping his poop."

she has personalized other traditional favorites as well. someone,
perhaps her grandmother, tried to teach her the "our father." her
version goes, "our pooper, who art in poopland, hallowed be thy
poop. thy poopdom poop, thy poop be pooped, on earth as it is in
poopland."

surely hemingway would feel one-upped. surely the second pooping
is at hand

a fortune teller told us blake would be our greatest sorrow and our
greatest joy. already, it is true.

NO RUSH

"my husband works nights," she says.

that throws new light on the subject.

night light.

"your husband ever arrive home unexpected?" i ask.

"only once," she says;
"bad case of stomach cramps."

i met her husband once.
it wasn't my idea.
he's twenty years younger than i am
and played semi-pro football for a steel mill.
he seems like a nice guy, but i suppose that
he's capable, like most of us,
of losing his composure under stress.

"maybe," i tell her, "we should wait
until after the flu season."

ILLUMINATION

Unlike everyone else in America,
I have never gotten laid at the laundromat.

Then again, it's my girl who does the laundry.

I'm going to have to end this poem right now—
something just occurred to me.

PHILLIP LOPATE

WALKING BACKWARDS

to Dziga Vertov

If time went backwards the bread would
return to the bakeries,
and newspapers to the typewriter keys' chapped lips,
the paper to the tree, crying and holding tight,
the maple syrup shuffling its feet up the bark

Mothers would know their children again:
The rock star, returning with an embarrassed kiss at the door,
would unpack his bag and go into his old room
with the green lamp and homework blotter and ham radio
to stare at the ceiling, then see if he can pick up Tokyo

The walleyed security guard, hallucinating
in the bank, returns to the spot where
his eyeballs first began to pull apart,
like college friends after graduation

The pensive receptionist pretending to look busy,
in bed the night before with her jobless boyfriend;
the lovers moving from climax to foreplay
from wetness to uncertainty, looking for a sign

The parachutist faltering and stretching his neck
like a turtle, not knowing which way is up

People we thought we had done with
would hit us like boomerangs:
girls walked away from at mixers,
dentists with dirty jokes, gym teachers,
blacks in pale green uniforms
wiping the counter at Chock Full of Nuts.
Rush hour faces recorded for no reason
than the wish that it might draw them back for a second look
this one a bonus, this time for pleasure —

I am not saying it would be so simple
I am not even saying it would all be worthwhile
but something I do know: the beef would get its intestines back
and I would get you back
resting my hand one more time
on the horn of your waist

and we would see snow
returning to the empty clouds
like a guilty wife, covering her husband
in ferocious white kisses to make him forget

THE WOMAN WHO CRIED FOR NOTHING

He introduced her to some friends in the street:
"This is a woman who cries for nothing."
Because after she flew to Sao Paulo to visit him
And the first day he was happy to see her;
And the second day he was pressed with life-worries;
And on the third day he was sad about
        taking a friend to the hospital
And the fourth day he threw his arms around her
        before everyone at the party and said,
        "How can we not live together?"
And on the fifth day he never called;
And on the sixth he listened deeply like an African to music;
And the seventh he proposed
        that they go to a hotel and make love;
And on the eighth he would not help her buy a bus ticket;
And on the last day when she met him in the street,
He looked serene and vital and offered to carry her bags,
She burst into tears;
And he asked, "What are you crying for?"
And she said, "For nothing."

IT'S PAINFUL GETTING LETTERS

It's painful getting letters from those
you love only a little, and who
think you're their best friend.
They write you four page laments and you
return one, three months later
full of hasty regrets.
You would like to love them completely
for what they are, as their mother loved them
(or didn't love them), but as you watch them flounder
in blandness and self-pity from one world capital to the next,
you can't escape the thought that they can do nothing for you.
unless it be to teach you a little more about
the sinking strategies of survival.
Each letter ends with a more passionately imagined rendezvous
which begins to sound like a threat:
"Have so much to tell in person —
I hope to come up through New Hampshire this July."
"Maybe we'll visit Denmark after all!"
So by now you can see inside out the day when
you two *will* be together, facing the stream
and pretending that beautiful Nature has made you silent.

THE BUM

Recently I saw a raggedy bum
take out his dick in the subway
and prepare to piss against the tile wall

Then he saw me and shrugged
as if to say, What can I do, I'm a failure
I can't hold it in

I should figure out a way to write this as a haiku

HANK MALONE

RECEIVING A LETTER FROM A FAMOUS POET

It flies into my house
& into my lobster-red hands, hot stuff
this letter from a famous man.
it's a kind of horizontal white torpedo

stamped with his leviathan name.
i play with the letter slowly.
it will be a letter of judgment
as powerful as religion & deep water.

what i call my soul seems to be squirming
despite my jokes about immortality.
a personal letter like this, from such a gladiator,
it's as close as i come to the voice of the earth.

I slit open the letter,
slashing.
ah, the words are kind. i drop my knife.
his voice from the top of the heap,
like a fishing hook loaded with bait,
it begs me to take my place alongside.
"the poems are better than ever," he says.
i bite into the hook as hard as i can.

PUBLISHING POEMS

somewhere in this world
someone is reading one of my poems.
later, he'll probably pick
his nose to death
& then call up his girlfriend.
"hello, phyllis?"
maybe they'll go out for fish & chips
or gumbo or vichyssoise
or wiener schnitzel.
"listen," he'll say,
"i just read this terrific poem."
& she'll be sleepy in his arms,
too tired to listen.
later, one of them will burp
into the darkness.
we are not fools.
poetry is a fragile bridge to be crossed.

10%

10% of americans are mentally ill.
one out of every ten americans
is an alcoholic.
10 out of a hundred are diabetics.
10% of our population
are child abusers.
one out of 10 americans
is malnourished.

& 10% of us are too fat,
10% suffer from pollution leading to cancer,
& one out of 10
abuses pills & prescription medication.
10% of us are compulsive gamblers
or workaholics headed for early heart attacks,
& 10% of us are unemployed & depressed.

90% of us
are hearing these statistics all the time
but we are too crazy
or drunk, or diabetic or abusive
or fat or cancerous or compulsive
to do anything about the mess.

so who will clean up
the statistics?
on my street there are shadows
that never leave the porch.

WITH THIS NEW POEM COMES FAME AND MY PICTURE ON THE COVERS OF MAGAZINES

& certain women will run up
& treat me like a movie star

suddenly i'll become handsome
& witty & perfect

& other men will hate my power
i'll become a famous victim of jealousy

& soon a fragrant light
will hover around my head

women will whisper about it
a great lover, the poet has become a saint!

later, the universe will change course
slowly it will approach me & revolve

it was inevitable
that i should die like this

famous grey hair
powerful baggy pants

JOSÉ MONTOYA

METAMORPHOSIS—OR, GUILTY WITH AN EXPLANATION

I explained
But they still
took almost everything

And the sightless lady
Apologized, but I
Had won!!

I walked out to
The Street unescorted
Y me fui por toda
La Efe and it was
Raining hard and I
Began to whistle
And I was the
cucaracha that
got away from
the raid of the
Black Flag—

Todo catiado, con
Una antena caida,
Pero libre and whistling—
My cockroach integrity
Intact!

FIVE, ALONE

Five Chicanos
On the nine o'clock
Special
To Vera Cruz
All together
Each alone

Camacho dreams
Of cool beaches
Y cocteles de
Ceviches

And Rita cradles
Robert's pale green
Death mask, reminder
Of last night's
Sour pulque

And Xavier complains

The train stops
Too much as he
Drinks Robert's
Brandy

And I sip a
Warm Corona
And eat a
Spicy torta
And I am reminded
I forgot to bring
Along some
Toilet paper

Bitch!
Bitch!
Bitch!

And we are not tourists
We almost convince ourselves
But the spirit hovers
It is there

And the conspiracy
We suspect continues
As the porter comes
Along warning of a
Hurricane weekend

The spirit hovers

We settle back
And we pass
Colonias cloaked
In nightness and
Nightmares of
Incredible
Poverty

And we try not
To see the distance
Lit-up with neon signs
For Firestone and
Of course Coca Cola

And the now dry
Ancient/modern
Lago de Texcoco
falls behind
As we head for
The mountains of
Orizaba and Cordoba
High, high and higher

Trying to forget
The neon malady
(Searching for roots
is so unclear!)

So we decide
To get drunk
With beer and
Brandy boiler-makers

And the lonesome whistle
From the engine

Snaking up ahead
Lends the night-trip
An air of adventure
    And the nostalgic
    fantasies produce
    a dizziness that's
    almost as pleasant
    as it is false and
    we brace to pretend—
    and we move toward the
    coast feeling weighted
    down

If only we didn't know
So much—Five Chicanos
On the nine o'clock
Special to Vera Cruz
    All together,
    each alone!

LISTEN

Up in the foothills
Not too far
From a Strategic
Air Command base
On a morning-star dawning
Of a sunrise sweat,
I was gradually startled
Gently by the alacrity
Of a million bird sounds.

Joyous music that had
Penetrated the rigors
Of the burning waters.

And my amazement
Was owed to the
Incredible realization
That the cooing of
Mourning doves, the
Chatter of blue jays
And the shrill versatility
of the mockingbirds
Had completely drowned out
The more familiar, unnatural
Noises of the B-52s
That in routine regularity
Virtually stun these hills
And beyond, even, all
Of the mornings
Of every day around
This time.

And I was greatly flattered
And thankful, knowing
I was finally re-learning
To hear. Listen!

HAROLD NORSE

IN NOVEMBER

In November I lost my food stamps, the computer said I did not
    exist
In November I lost my best friend who said I did not exist
In November I lost my manuscripts and felt as if I did not exist
In November I sent 2 postcards to my mother who wrote back
    saying she had not heard from me and DID I STILL EXIST?
In November I paid the telephone bill and received a final notice
    for the non-payment
In November my girlfriend accused me of unreality and infrequency
    with a tendency to dematerialize on weekends and holidays
    even Jewish ones and stormed out leaving a sinkful of dirty
    dishes and linen blackened by her feet, souvenirs of blood
    and tobacco burns
In November my checks bounced, mail stopped arriving, the toilet
    clogged, the cat choked, my poems were rejected, I got worms,
    the clap and psoriasis of the anus, all I needed was an
    earthquake to prove my destiny was not to be overlooked,
    and one was long overdue according to the latest reliable
    heavenly and scientific sources
In November I looked for all my published works in City Lights
    Bookstore and found only my early translations of Belli,
    I did not exist on the bookshelves altho' a thesis to prove
    that I *did* exist was written by some kid in Arkansas, 300
    pages that nobody ever read called *Orpheus Unacclaimed:*
    Harold Norse, So What?
In November I gave a poetry reading which was so well advertised
    one day in advance that 5 people actually came, 4 of them
    drunk and cantankerous, the fifth had lost his way to the
    toilet, and one of the drunks kept asking, "Tell me how
    to win! I'm sick of being a loser!" and I answered from
    years of eminence: "Be invisible!"
In November when I crossed the street with the light a grayhaired
    man in a Cadillac looking like Spiro Agnew tried to run me
    down and swore because he missed me, something about Law
    and Order
In November I screamed at the neighbors upstairs who played
    stereo hard rock all day and night that crashed thru the
    floorboards but they said I was a liar it was music not noise
    and I was a fink for complaining and the one who practiced
    karate over my bedroom from midnite until 3 am said why
    didn't I take up yoga and gain deliverance from bad karma so
    they went on playing their rock and hammering on the floor
    and stomping in boots and breaking bricks until 4 am as if I did
    not exist and
In November I gave thanks for all my blessings without a turkey,
    with one good ear, high cholesterol, 59¢, 145 lbs. and 2 good
    balls.

TO MOHAMMED ON OUR JOURNEYS

I was the tourist
el simpático
and your brother offered you
and also himself

I forgot about your brother
and we took a flat in the Marshan
with reed mats and one water tap
about a foot from the floor
and we smoked hasheesh
and ate well and loved well
and left for the south
Essaouira, Fez, Marrakech
and got to Taroudant
thru the mountains
and bought alabaster kif bowls
for a few dirhams and watched
the dancing boys in desert cafés
kissing old Arabs and sitting on their
laps, dancing with kohl eyes, and
heard the music down in Joujouka
in the hills under the stars
the ancient ceremony, Pan pipes
fierce in white moonlight
and the white walls with hooded figures
stoned on kif for eight nights
and the goatboy in a floppy hat
scared us, beating the air
with a stick, beating whoever came close,
Father of Skins, goat god,
and the flutes maddened us
and we slept together in huts

San Francisco, 7.xi.72

VERLAINE DIED HERE

How many times I have passed this house
watched the curtains against the shutters
and the plaque on the gray façade
telling the year of your death
Verlaine
in this room above the bookshop on the
rue Descartes—ailing street
of sad *clochards* . . .
I have stood thinking
of your hurricane of junk and mud
the noise of cafés and buses and dripping walls
with that half-hearted paradise at the end
wondering who is behind those closed windows
a laundress perhaps
someone to whom your name is only a name
like you stuck on that sandbar where voyages stop

WE BUMPED OFF YOUR FRIEND THE POET ⟵ *Political*

Based on a review by Cyril Connolly, Death in Granada, *on the last days of Garcia Lorca, The Sunday Times (London), May 20, 1973.*

We bumped off your friend the poet
with the big fat head this morning

We left him in a ditch
I fired 2 bullets into his ass
for being queer

I was one of the people
who went to get Lorca
and that's what I said to Rosales

My name is Ruiz Alonso
ex-typographer
Right-wing deputy
alive and kicking
Falangist to the end

Nobody bothers me
I got protection
the Guardia Civil are my friends

Because he was a poet
was he better than anyone else?

He was a goddam fag
and we were sick and tired
of fags in Granada

The black assassination squads
kept busy
liquidating professors
doctors lawyers students
like the good old days of the Inquisition!

General Queipo de Llano
had a favorite phrase
"Give him coffee, plenty of coffee!"

When Lorca was arrested
we asked the General what to do
"Give him coffee, plenty of coffee!"

So we took him out in the hills and shot him
I'd like to know what's wrong with that
he was a queer with Leftist leanings

Didn't he say
I don't believe in political frontiers?

Didn't he say
The capture of Granada in 1492
by Ferdinand and Isabella
was a disastrous event?

Didn't he call Granada *a wasteland*
peopled by the worst bourgeoisie in Spain?

a queer Communist poet!

General Franco owes me a medal
for putting 2 bullets up his ass

YOUR CROOKED BEAUTY . . .

Your crooked beauty, Hugo,
maims us. You are all
that hurts. Taking us
off guard with your virile
grace, good looks. But
you're crooked, you're bad news.
So you brought in the new
year that already had no good
in it for me, exiled
from a loveless country, took
what you wanted from its hiding place
among dirty clothing — 30,000 liras —
then ground your teeth. I saw madness,
Hugo, death in your heroic
stony features, bones more enormous
than clubs, murderous jaws, the unseeing
statue stare of senselessness. Now
what's the use? At that price
your beauty is too expensive, leaving
neither regard for feelings
nor the rent.

Rome, New Year's Day, 1954

IN THE CAFES

(After Cavafy)

In the cafés, smoky and noisy,
and the loud bars with their screeching
and punk rock madness that deafens me
I'm bored. I've never cared for
these trashy joints. But they're good for drowning
persistent echoes of Keith. Quite suddenly
he left, without warning, for the proud
owner of two Porsches and a big house in Marin,
a hot tub and swimming pool. Keith, I don't doubt,
has tender feelings for me still. Yet I'm sure
he has learned to develop tender feelings
for a man with two Porsches. I live
in squalor. But what stays fresh
and sweet, what keeps me going, is
that for two whole months I had Keith,
the most desirable youth
on Polk Street. None
could compare with him. In my drab flat
with a view of trash cans and parking lots
he lived with me, a warm
affectionate lover—there was surely more to him
than meets the eye—mine not for a mansion
and two fast Porsches.

San Francisco, 29.ix.85

YOU MUST HAVE BEEN A SENSATIONAL BABY

1

I love your eyebrows, said one.
the distribution of your bodyhair
is sensational. what teeth, said two.
your mouth is cocaine, said three.
your lips, said four, look like sexual organs.
they are, I said.
as I got older features thickened.
the body grew flabby. then
thin in the wrong places. they
all shut up or spoke about life.

2

a pair of muscular calves
drove me crazy today.
I studied their size, their shape,
their suntanned hairiness. I spoke
to the owner of them. are you
a dancer? I asked. oh no,
I was born with them, he said.
you must have been a sensational baby,
I said. he went back to his newspaper.
I went back to his calves.
he displayed them mercilessly.
he was absolutely heartless.
men stole secret looks at them.
women pretended he was a table.
they all had a pained expression.
he went on reading the Sports Page.
his thighs were even more cruel
thrust brutally from denim shorts.
the whole place trembled with lust.

SHARON OLDS

THE SISTERS OF SEXUAL TREASURE

As soon as my sister and I got out of our
mother's house, all we wanted to
do was fuck, obliterate
her tiny sparrow body and narrow
grasshopper legs. The men's bodies
were like our father's body! The massive
hocks, flanks, thighs, elegant
knees, long tapered calves —
we could have him there, the steep forbidden
buttocks, backs of the knees, the cock
in our mouth, ah the cock in our mouth.
        Like explorers who
discover a lost city, we went
nuts with joy, undressed the men
slowly and carefully, as if
uncovering buried artifacts that
proved our theory of the lost culture:
that if Mother said it wasn't there,
it was there.

THE MISSING BOY

(for Etan Patz)

Every time we take the bus
my son sees the picture of the missing boy.
He looks at it like a mirror — the dark
blond hair, the pale skin,
the blue eyes, the electric-blue sneakers with
slashes of jagged gold. But of course that
kid is little, only six and a half,
an age when things can happen to you,
when you're not really safe, and Gabriel is seven,
practically full grown — why, he would
tower over that kid if they could
find him and bring him right here on this bus and
stand them together. He sways in the silence
wishing for that, the tape on the picture
gleaming over his head, beginning to
melt at the center and curl at the edges as it
ages. At night, when I put him to bed,
my son holds my hand tight
and says he's sure that kid's all right,
nothing to worry about, he just
hopes he's getting the food he likes,
not just any old food, but the food
he likes the most, the food he is used to.

THE TALK

In the dark square wooden room at noon
the mother had a talk with her daughter.
The rudeness could not go on, the meanness
to her little brother, the selfishness.
The 8-year-old sat on the bed
in the corner of the room, her irises dark as
the last drops of something, her firm
face melting, reddening,
silver flashes in her eyes like distant
bodies of water glimpsed through woods.
She took it and took it and broke, crying out
I hate being a person! diving
into the mother
as if
into
a deep pond — and she cannot swim,
the child cannot swim.

FIVE-YEAR-OLD BOY

Gabriel at five is leaning on the world
the way a factory foreman leans on
a slow worker. As he talks, he holds
a kitchen strainer in his hand. At the end of
the conversation, the handle is twisted,
the mesh burst — he looks down at it
amazed. Mysterious things are always
happening in his hands. As he tells a story,
he dances backwards. Nothing is safe
near this boy. He stands on the porch, peeing
into the grass, watching a bird
fly around the house, and ends up
pissing on the front door. Afterwards he
twangs his penis. Long after
the last drops fly into the lawn,
he stands there gently rattling his dick,
his face full of intelligence,
his white, curved forehead slightly
puckered in thought, his eyes clear,
gazing out over the pond,
his mouth firm and serious;
abstractedly he shakes himself
once more
and the house collapses
to the ground behind him.

I GO BACK TO MAY 1937

I see them standing at the formal gates of their colleges,
I see my father strolling out
under the ochre sandstone arch, the
red tiles glinting like bent
plates of blood behind his head, I
see my mother with a few light books at her hip
standing at the pillar made of tiny bricks with the
wrought-iron gate still open behind her, its
sword-tips black in the May air,
they are about to graduate, they are about to get married,
they are kids, they are dumb, all they know is they are
innocent, they would never hurt anybody.
I want to go up to them and say Stop,
don't do it — she's the wrong woman,
he's the wrong man, you are going to do things
you cannot imagine you would ever do,
you are going to do bad things to children,
you are going to suffer in ways you never heard of,
you are going to want to die. I want to go
up to them there in the late May sunlight and say it,
her hungry pretty blank face turning to me,
her pitiful beautiful untouched body,
his arrogant handsome blind face turning to me,
his pitiful beautiful untouched body,
but I don't do it. I want to live. I
take them up like the male and female
paper dolls and bang them together
at the hips like chips of flint as if to
strike sparks from them, I say
Do what you are going to do, and I will tell about it.

LATE

The mist is blowing across the yard
like smoke from a battle.
I am so tired of the women doing dishes
and how smart the men are, and how I want to
bite their mouths and feel their hard cocks against me.

The mist moves, over the bushes
bright with poison ivy and black
berries like stones. I am tired of the children,
I am tired of the laundry, I want to be great.

The fog pours across the underbrush in silence.
We are sealed in. The only way out is through
fire, and I do not want a single
hair of a single head singed.

SIMON ORTIZ

UPSTATE

Coming from Montreal
we stopped at a roadside place.
She had to use the restroom
and I stepped into the tavern.
A man, surly white drunk, told me,
"I know an Indian who dances nearby."
He wanted to show me, cursed me
because I was sullen
and didn't want to see.
She came and saved me.
I said, "It's a good thing you're white."
And she was hurt, angry.
It's an old story.
On the wall was a stuffed deerhead,
fluff falling out, blank sad eyes.
We drove madly out of the parking lot
and she didn't say anything
until we finally arrived in Vermont.

We were tired of being in the car,
our bodies and spirits cramped.
We ate in a small town.
We drove to a hillside.
The weather was muggy and hot.
I talked crummy to her, made love,
she cried, I felt sorry and bad.
I get crazy sometimes and impossible
I've heard.
              It rained hard that night.
The lights of the town below
shimmering through the rain into me.
All night long, I was lonely
and bothered by New England Indian ghosts.

AND ANOTHER ONE:

                One time,
four people were eating together.
They saw Pehrru approaching them.
He was coming up the road.

One of them said,
"There comes Pehrru.
Don't anyone invite him to sit down and eat.
He's much of a liar."
The four kept on eating.

Pehrru got to where they were,
and he said, "Guwahzee."
"Dawah eh," they answered,
and they kept on eating.
Nobody invited Pehrru to sit down and eat.

"Wah trou yatawah?" Pehrru asked.
And they answered, "Hah uh, wahstou yatawah."
("Are you eating?"
"Yes, we're eating.")
Pehrru stood around watching them eat.

To make conversation,
one of the four asked,
"Where are you coming from?"
And Pehrru said,
"Oh, I'm coming from nowhere special."

After a bit more silence, another asked,
"Dze shru tu ni, Pehrru?"
And Pehrru answered,
"Oh, as usual I don't know much of anything."
The four kept on eating
and Pehrru kept standing, watching them eat.

And then he said,
"Oh wait, I do know a bit of something,"
and he paused until he was sure
they were waiting for him to go on,
and then he said,
"When I was coming here, I saw some cows."

Pretending to show little interest,
one said, "Oh well, one usually sees
some cows around."

And Pehrru said, "Yes, yes that's true,
Well, one of them had just given birth
to some calves."

And one of them said,
"Oh well, you know, usually cows
give birth to calves."

"The cow was feeding her calves,"
Pehrru said.

"Oh well, that's what cows usually do,
feed their calves," one of the four said.

And then Pehrru said,
"The cow had given birth to five calves.
One of them, beloved, was just standing around,
looking hungry, not feeding because
as you know, cows usually only have four nipples."

And the four, realizing the meaning
of Pehrru's story, looked at each other
and said,
"Shtsu dzeshu, Pehrru. Sit down and eat."
Smiling, Pehrru joined them in eating.

When it was time to get a meal,
Pehrru was known to be a shrewd man.

MY FATHER'S SONG

Wanting to say things,
I miss my father tonight.
His voice, the slight catch,
the depth from his thin chest,
the tremble of emotion
in something he has just said
to his son, his song:

We planted corn one Spring at Acu—
we planted several times
but this one particular time
I remember the soft damp sand
in my hand.

My father had stopped at one point
to show me an overturned furrow;
the plowshare had unearthed
the burrow nest of a mouse
in the soft moist sand.

Very gently, he scooped tiny pink animals
into the palm of his hand
and told me to touch them.
We took them to the edge
of the field and put them in the shade
of a sand moist clod.

I remember the very softness
of cool and warm sand and tiny alive mice
and my father saying things.

BONY

My father brought that dog home
in a gunny sack.

The reason we called it Bony
was because it was skin and bones.

It was a congenital problem
or something that went way back
in its dog's history.

We loved it without question,
its history and ours.

DAN PROPPER

ODE TO THE CINEMA

(for Nathaniel West)

The huge images
move upon the immense white screen:
we are at the movies, and there is conflict.
Always there is conflict at the movies,
and we sit, large replicas
of the animals we once were as children,
and we laugh, and weep, and scream,
and we pick our noses, and we
stuff ourselves with incredibly tempting
useless food, and we throw everything
on the floor, because we are At The Movies.

Look! Cardinal Richelieu plots again!
Look! A gigantic manlike beast
rises from the swamp and
crunches human beings like radishes!
Look! Moses sees God, accompanied
by an organ. Look again! It's God Himself,
played by Charlton Heston.

Look again! Look again!
The movies go on, the movies are eternal.
What's playing at the movies?
The Movies are playing at the movies!

Did you know that the insane asylums
are full of people who think
they're Napoleon? Napoleon himself
thought he was Jesus. Jesus, in turn,
thought that he was God.
What does God Think?
Where does it all end?
It ends in the Movies!

Here! The cavalry is massacring the Indians!
Here! The Indians are torturing a soldier!
Here, a friendly old priest
is spooning soup into an exhausted alcoholic.
Here, for some reason, is a close-up
of the world's biggest pair of tits!
The show's only begun: here's "Romeo And Juliet,"
played by Joe Namath and Barbra Streisand!
Here's the United Nations, played by John Carradine!
Here's "The Invisible Man," played by The Holy Ghost!
Joan Crawford and the Houston Philharmonic
starring in "Sodom And Gomorrah"! What a show!

The endless figures parade across the immense
panorama of the screen, immortal, impassioned,
and compassionate upon the vast horizon.

Here's a torrential storm lashing
the fear-crazed natives of a paradisical isle!
Here! Surrounded by oafs, dolts, and louts,
a solitary genius invents the wheel!
Icarus flies! Ulysses trips!
Get another bag of peanuts,
we haven't seen anything yet!
Here comes the Peloponnesian War!
There's "The Conquest of Peru," in E-flat.
Ben Franklin and Thomas Jefferson
are drinking ale in Cinemascope.
Are you tired? Here's a nice nostalgic
Faulknerian story about stomping around
in the woods, in the rain, drunk
carrying shotguns and mumbling something
or other about Niggers and Yankees.
Here's The World's Handsomest Man,
and his wife, The World's Most Beautiful Woman,
and their love for each other,
The World's Most Perfect Example Of Love.

Here, in the dark palace of dreaming,
in the cushioned, insulated, encapsulate
nave of the imagination, is gentleness,
ferocity, courage, love, honor, magnanimity,
cowardice, humility, stupidity, cruelty,
vengefulness, mercy, and righteousness!
Here is ecstasy and shame!

Here is man attacking a woman
with a gigantic knife! Here is a woman
attacking a child with a cup of acid!
Here is a child attacking a village
with burning gasoline!, at the movies.

Here's a documentary: President Kennedy
is being shot, again, and again, and again,
in slow-motion, in grainy close-ups,
at normal speed. Here's World War II,
with Glenn Ford, Richard Widmark,
John Wayne, Richard Jaeckel, Alan Ladd,
Frederick March, Gregory Peck,
Robert Mitchum, Clark Gable,
William Holden, Trevor Howard, and Lassie.
Here're the Jews wandering in the desert
40 years, it only takes 3 minutes.

Here's Franklin Delano Roosevelt saving America,
and Winston Churchill saving England, and
Josef Stalin saving Russia, and Adolf Hitler
saving Germany, and Kwame Nkrumah saving Ghana,
and Chiang Kai Shek saving China, and Fidel Castro
saving Cuba, DeGaulle saving France, Nasser
saving Egypt, and Ho Chi Minh saving Vietnam
at the movies, at the movies,
at the movies, at the movies, at the movies!

Children, let me slip it to you
really quick and gentle.
The Movies are merely a great opportunity
to holler "Theatre!" in a fiery crowd.

Do you want to see God?

Don't look in the movies,
because God absolutely
does not go to the movies.
If you had any sense, neither would you.

Tonight? Tonight is
Marlon Brando and Anna Magnani
in "The Ramayana." Hurry up,
we don't want to miss the beginning.

11/30—12/7/72

A CHAGALL (#5)

A mermaid! Oh sweet
Christ Almighty,
a mermaid, and
with red hair!
And floating in air,
no water, high above
a line of date palms,
high above a road
and a row of houses,
and high above
a floating fish
himself above
everything else
except the sun,
gently holding
a huge bouquet of
flowers, red, yellow,
and white, they float too,
and her tail
yellow, orange,
white and blue,
and white clouds
in a pale ultramarine sky,
barely delineated,
and large titties,
she has giant
straight-thrusting titties,
you'd never believe them
on a girl, let alone
on a mermaid.

7/2/68

ONE, TWO, MANY POETRY READINGS

Always three in red and six in black;
always at least one lined face;
always a few on display;
usually a headache, and absolutely always
a hangover;
2 or 3 God-struck ones,
2 blond kids hoping to get laid,
6 ex-junkies, 4 homosexuals,
17 bi-sexuals, and 2 sad celibates;
possibly four with talent, all
secretly knowing themselves the nation's greatest;
6 shameless amateurs;
always two dropped-out musicians:
"I used to play alto,"
"I played drums";
one ex-beauty, one nervous lady with short hair,
one male late-adolescent sexual posturer;
always a babbling refugee from hallucinogens;
one with a long poem called "The Ultimate List,"
one meshugineh talking about corduroy tulips,
and one Visiting Star.

1/18/73

KAREN SNOW

SECRETARY

Secretary's just her cover.
She's been hired to revive my husband.

Gone are his headaches;
going, his paper shuffler slump.
He swoops into the kitchen
at five-thirty like something
that's been whirled by a dervish.

Just when I was resigned to being boxed
in for my remaining reclusive years —
my enabler and I parallel in padded
recliners, grumbling cozily
over books and bifocals,

he has this satori.

Our box is buffeted with new hobbies.
Tum tum goes mallet on chisel.
He's releasing devilish grins
from chunks of apple wood. Sally
found him the mask book at a garage
sale, brought the aromatic wood
from her orchard. His shirt
has started to swell at the shoulders.
His hands grip things. Saturday he
spaded two deep holes in the yard,
mulched them lushly, and stuffed them
with balled saplings.

He's fifty.

Sally's thirty, married, mother of three.
Picnic polaroids plus telephone contralto
add up to a country music performer.

It's platonic.
I almost wrote playtonic. She's his
friend, and that's what I never was.

They lunch together in ethnic restaurants,
usually with colleagues. Always, Malcolm
relays, it turns into a circus.

While cloistered in my kitchen
with yogurt and granola, the table raps
with their laughter, the curtains twitch
with a silly aside, the white wall flushes.

I hate this.
Months after homemade meditation
had made of me a hung sock
into which The Muse was slipping coiled
verbs and metaphors, I'm switched

to this lower channel.

Around two o'clock, when Malcolm phones
to inquire about the mail, my fatigue,
my backache, his voice sounds so smiley
I picture a piano keyboard talking.

"We had lunch at the casino," he trills.
I dare not reply: *I know, I saw it all.*

Not *all.* I don't want to exaggerate.
It's not a telecast. It's more of a single
frame, a split second snatch, usually
with sound.

Clairvoyance it's called. It's quite
common. The cheap kind of common,
and I hate it

— hate the feelings, I mean, that boil
out of it.

A scrupulously private person,
too self-contained to eavesdrop
or to follow the twists of a spy plot,

I find myself hooked into this noonsy
network. Five hours a week— Ten—
They dally over dessert. Make it forty-five
hours— I'm a novice in a high wire act,
jounced by a professional from net
to trapeze to net to tightrope.

I'm all adrenalin.

Not that I'm green to the green game.
Hindsight flashes a shadowed office
where a professor croons literary suggestions
to this sylph with a nimbus of flaxen hair,
violet sash, sweetly skewed mind.
Outside, in a chilled car, his wife
and children wait. And wait. Her pangs
are my applause.

Now I'm on the pang side.

You bitch I blurted the other noon
via my bean sprouts when the snatch
disclosed Malcolm whooping at her pun.
May something bad happen to you.

Minutes later I apologized.

Too late. Her son was struck
by a car while pedaling his tricycle.
When Malcolm phoned at two he said,
sepulchrally, Sally had been called
to the hospital.

Naturally I grew edgy about our son
at college. The meditation book warns
of *the echo.* My hackles know.
And being Catholic, Sally
has all that protection, whereas I'm
open to the elements.

It turned out to be a fractured collar
bone. Our son wrote that he was down

with a cold. I hope that wraps it up.

Today is my birthday. Fifty-two.
Oh dear. I saw Great Geisha lunge
across the table and grab Malcolm
by the tie. "Give your tootsie some-
thing luscious, you hear?" *A book
of poems, please*, I telepathized.
Then they were in a greenhouse where
they selected— She selected a plant
with plush leaves and plump buds
and a large crimson flower like a ruf-
fled funnel.   Next they were in Mal-
colm's car chortling back to the office,
the blossom in Sally's lap bobbling.

At five-thirty that ruffled red thing
came jiggling into the kitchen
just below sheepish tie and piano grin.
Bam! went the ceiling. "What's that?"
Malcolm asked. *Jealousy!* I almost
screamed. "Sounded like a gunshot," he mused.
Bing! went the wainscotting.
Always in pairs, Jung noted: one plus
the echo. And I was grateful for the
pause to intellectualize.

"Happy birthday, Honey." Malcolm
was gobbling my face as if he'd forgotten
for the moment who I was. "I'll bet,"
he panted, "you never saw a gloxinia before."

"Well—" I ventured, firming my grip
on the trapeze, "I saw one once, but I
didn't catch its name—"

GARY SNYDER

CARTAGENA

Rain and thunder beat down and flooded the streets
We danced with Indian girls in a bar,
      water half-way to our knees,
The youngest one slipped down her dress and danced
      bare to the waist,
The big negro deckhand made out with his girl on his lap
      in a chair her dress over her eyes
Coca-cola and rum, and rainwater all over the floor.
In the glittering light I got drunk and reeled through the rooms,
And cried, "Cartagena! swamp of unholy loves!"
And wept for the Indian whores who were younger than me,
      and I was eighteen,
And splashed after the crew down the streets wearing sandals bought
    at a stall
And got back to the ship, dawn came,
      we were far out at sea.

NANSEN

I found you on a rainy morning
After a typhoon
In a bamboo grove at Daitoku-ji.
Tiny wet rag with a
Huge voice, you crawled under the fence
To my hand. Left to die.
I carried you home in my raincoat.
"Nansen, cheese!" you'd shout an answer
And come running.
But you never got big.
Bandy-legged bright little dwarf—
Sometimes not eating, often coughing
Mewing bitterly at inner twinge.

Now, thin and older, you won't eat
But milk and cheese. Sitting on a pole
In the sun. Hardy with resigned
Discontent.
You just weren't made right. I saved you,
And your three-year life has been full
Of mild, steady pain.

I WENT INTO THE MAVERICK BAR

I went into the Maverick Bar
In Farmington, New Mexico.
And drank double shots of bourbon
   backed with beer.
My long hair was tucked up under a cap
I'd left the earring in the car.

Two cowboys did horseplay
  by the pool tables,
A waitress asked us
    where are you from?
a country-and-western band began to play
"We don't smoke Marijuana in Muskokie"
And with the next song,
   a couple began to dance.

They held each other like in High School dances
   in the fifties;
I recalled when I worked in the woods
   and the bars of Madras, Oregon.
That short-haired joy and roughness —
   America — your stupidity.
I could almost love you again.

We left — onto the freeway shoulders —
   under the tough old stars —
In the shadow of bluffs
   I came back to myself,
To the real work, to
   "What is to be done."

TWO IMMORTALS

Sitting on a bench by the Rogue River, Oregon, looking at a land-form map. Two older gents approached me and one, with baseball cap, began to sing: "California Here I Come" — he must have seen the license. Asked me if I'd ever heard of Texas Slim. Yes. And he said the song "If I Had the Wings of an Angel" was his, had been writ by him, "I was in the penitentiary." "Let me shake your hand! That's a good song" I said, and he showed me his hand: faint blue traces of tattoo on the back, on the bent fingers. And if I hit you with this hand it's L-O-V-E. And if I hit you with this hand it's H-A-T-E.

His friend, in a red and black buffalo check jacket, stuck his hand out, under my nose, missing the forefinger. "How'd I lose that!" "How?" "An axe!"

Texas Slim said "I'm just giving him a ride. Last year his wife died." The two ambled off, chuckling, as Kai and Gen came running back up from the banks of Rogue River, hands full of round river stones.

Looking at the map, it was the space inside the loop of the upper Columbia, eastern Washington plateau country. "Channelled Scab-lands."

AN AUTUMN MORNING IN SHOKU

Last night watching the Pleiades,
Breath smoking in the moonlight,
Bitter memory like vomit
Choked my throat.
I unrolled a sleeping bag
On mats on the porch
Under thick autumn stars.
In dream you appeared
(Three times in nine years)
Wild, cold, and accusing.
I woke shamed and angry:
The pointless wars of the heart.
Almost dawn. Venus and Jupiter.
The first time I have
Ever seen them close.

NO SHOES NO SHIRT NO SERVICE

Padding down the street, the
Bushmen, the Paiute, the Cintas Largas
        are refused.
The queens of Crete,
the waiting-ladies of the King of Bundelkhand.
Tārā is kept out,
Bare-breasted on her lotus throne.

        (officially, no one goes through
        unofficially, horses go through,
        carriages go through—)

The barefoot shepherds, the bare-chested warriors

        (What is this gate,
        wide as a highway
        that only mice can enter?)

The cow passed through the window nicely—
Only the tail got stuck,

And the soils of this region will be fertile again
After another round of volcanoes
Nutrient ash—
        Shiva's dancing feet
        (No shoes)

U

fighting in the street, she
to the baby/he livid
g her/trying to wrest the kid
away/the baby's bald pink head
in danger of being brained
bloody on the pavement/I tried
to stop him/she's crazy, he says
she's been with another guy/she
took the baby/she's crazy

and no doubt she is/off her
tranquilizers/nuts/but so is he
and I leave them/gut twisted/
remembering fights with you
in streets/rooms/on subway platforms
public places/my scalp split open
in Holland/knife wounds in Westchester and
Berlin/terrible brawls in
The Bronx

and suddenly it hit me how
we must have looked/so
pitiful/so full of pain
so scared

*chopped
urgent
he's getting
straight to the
point.
conversational
diction.
realization*

THE FAVOR

You did me
a favor
pushing me
out the window

I learned
how to
fly

ALL-PURPOSE APOLOGY POEM

As a responsible adult I must admit
my guilt.

I did it.

Not the weather, not
my wife, not some 'mood'
that mysteriously entered as I slept.

I did it.

'Guilt' may be too strong a word
but, in fact, I did the thing,
I made it happen.

No outside cause. No god, no devil.
No accident of fate, no drug or drink
or pill.

I did it.

I used my mind, I moved my hands
and arms and legs, 'twas me who
dood it.

I broke the _____, I ruined the _____,
I said the thing not said,
I was insensitive, I was at fault.

I did it.

I drove the car, I dropped the dish,
I lost the key, I swung my fist,
I tore the page, I spilled the beer

I did it.

I was mean. I was stupid.
I was petty. I was cold.

Check one.

I did it.

Not you, not ten other guys,
not my parents, teachers, political
leaders, not even the capitalists or Russians.

Not my stars. Nor the moon
or sun or winds and tides.

Not my dog or my cat
or my bird.

It was me. Me. Me.

I'm ashamed. I'm sorry, I won't
do it again, what a fool I was!

I did it.
Mea culpa.

It was ME!

AL ZOLYNAS

THE ZEN OF HOUSEWORK

I look over my own shoulder
down my arms
to where they disappear under water
into hands inside pink rubber gloves
moiling among dinner dishes.

My hands lift a wine glass,
holding it by the stem and under the bowl.
It breaks the surface
like a chalice
rising from a medieval lake.

Full of the grey wine
of domesticity, the glass floats
to the level of my eyes.
Behind it, through the window
above the sink, the sun, among
a ceremony of sparrows and bare branches,
is setting in Western America.

I can see thousands of droplets
of steam — each a tiny spectrum — rising
from my goblet of grey wine.
They sway, changing directions
constantly — like a school of playful fish,
or like the sheer curtain
on the window to another world.

Ah, grey sacrament of the mundane!

OUR CAT'S FASCINATION WITH WATER

I wake to his weight on my chest, his half-closed eyes saying it's
time to get up, human. In the bathroom, I turn on the faucet in the
tub for him, the way I have most mornings the last two years. He
jumps in. The black flames of his eyes widen. Again, he can't believe
it, can't believe the silver cord hanging from the silver faucet, can't
believe he lives in a world that gives him the same, new gift each
morning; can't believe it, so he has to touch it, and then can't believe
his paw goes right through it, and has to touch it again and again;
and I, looking at his lost eyes, the wet paw, the tail flicking on the
white porcelain, my untouchable other self on the silver surface of
the mirror, can't believe it either.

132

THE HAT IN THE SKY

After the war
after I was born,
my father's hobby
(perhaps his obsession)
was photography.
It seems new fathers
often turn to photography.
But he took pictures
of many things besides me,
as if he felt it all slipping
away and wanted to hold it
forever. In one of the many
shoe-boxes full of photos
in my father's house, one
sticks in my mind.
It's a snapshot
of a black hat in mid-air,
the kind of hat fashionable
in the forties, a fedora —
one Bogie would wear.
Someone has thrown it
into the air —
perhaps my father himself,
perhaps someone in an exuberant moment
in a crowd. It's still there,
hanging in the sky
as ordinary and impossible
as a painting by Magritte,
and it's impossible
how it wrenches my heart, somehow.
At odd moments in my life,
that hat appears
for no discernible reason.

A NIGHTMARE CONCERNING PRIESTS

They whirl down the aisles;
the congregation applauds.
Frankly, I'm frightened.
From the pulpit the bishop
shows us his armpits.
They are hairless
like a female trapeze artist's.
When he speaks, his teeth
click like dice and white hosts
tumble from his mouth.
The people don't mind;
they count it a blessing.
From up on the cross,
high above the altar, Christ
calls to the multitude
for someone to please,
please scratch his nose.
Twelve nuns in the front row
gaze at him sweetly.
One polishes
a wedding band against her habit.

ONE MAN'S POISON

In the men's room in the basement
of the Saint Paul Public Library
a man hands me a pint of whiskey
and asks me to open
the son of a bitch it's on too tight.
I do and am embarrassed
that I can so easily:
my mother's jars, my wife's jars
are tougher than this.
By a perverse alchemy
this man's wrists have turned to milk.
He's an alcoholic he says
and knows he may die any day now
but adds proudly
I ain't hurting no one but myself.
He thanks me and offers me a drink
as I stand in front of the urinal
trying to piss. I, standing in front
of a urinal in the basement of the Saint Paul
Public Library, politely decline — somehow
not much in my life
has prepared me for this.
Upstairs, I don't check out any books.

DOODLES

We find them around
the leavings of telephone
conversations clinging
to addresses, appointments;

around the notes
of committee members,
judges; in the margins
of grocery lists and aborted

poems. They are always
on the edges, sliding
away like vitreous floaters
when we try to see

them clearly. For all their ubiquity,
they are humble and basic:
flowers, stars, stick-men,
uncomplicated by the rules of

perspective and modeling.
They leave the loud shout
of the third dimension to Art.

They are content to whisper.

THE SAME AIR
— *for Guy Murchie,* The Seven Mysteries of Life

that moves
through me and you
through the waving branches
of the bronchial tree
through veins
through the heart
the same air
that fills balloons
that carries voices
full of lies and truths
and half-truths
that holds up the wings of butterflies
humming birds eagles hang gliders 747's
the same air
that sits like a dull relative
on humid lakes
in Minnesota in summer
the same air
trapped in vintage champagne
in old bicycle tires lost tennis balls
the air inside the tanks of skin divers
inside a vial in a sarcophagus
in a tomb in a pyramid
buried beneath the sand
the same air
inside your freezer
wrapping its cold arms
around your t.v. dinners
the same air that supports you
that supports me
the same air that moves through us
that we move through
the same air frogs croak with
cattle bellow with
monks meditate with and on
the same air we moan with
in pleasure or in pain

the breath I'm taking now
will be in China in two weeks
my lungs have passed an atom
of oxygen that passed through the lungs
of Socrates or Plato
or Lao-tse or Buddha
or Walt Disney or Ronald Reagan
or a starving child in Somalia
or certainly you
you right here right now
yes certainly you
the same air
the very same air

THE HOMECOMING

After years away from the city
you return and find your father
in a family album suddenly grown
younger, grown younger like the cops
in squad cars patrolling the streets,
licensed teenagers, the faint
figure-eight imprints of prophylactics
still in their bulky wallets.
He is younger than you now,
knows less than you, though he tries
to hide it with a cocked head
and arched eyebrows. Your mother
a virgin beside him with a virgin's
smile. You are in that smile
the way the sun is in a coffee bean
or a good cigar, waiting
for the magic to release you.
And you are in your father's house now,
years later, somehow still a child,
but strangely father to the man at last,
waiting for the magic to release you.

A POLITICAL POEM

At the corner cafe
where I sometimes eat
I ordered a raw egg
broken into a cup
no toast no coffee.
I tossed that egg down
my throat like a cossack
taking vodka.
I did it for shock
value, for the value of the shock.
I did it for the waitress
for my mother for the sunny siders
and hard boilers the over easys.
I did it for those hopelessly
scrambled by America.

THE CANDLE ON THE URINAL, NEW DELHI

After a steaming day of temples, mosques, pillars and towers, we
return to the Hotel Rajdoot. I go into the "Gents" on the ground
floor. There's been a power outage and the only light in the
cavernous space comes from a burnt-down candle on top of the
urinal. It pushes its small light against the looming walls and ceiling.
I step up to the unexpected altar, present myself to the softly
glowing porcelain and watch, as if for the first time again, the sacred
water flow.

LOVE IN THE CLASSROOM

— for my students

Afternoon. Across the garden, in Green Hall,
someone begins playing the old piano —
a spontaneous piece, amateurish and alive,
full of a simple, joyful melody.
The music floats among us in the classroom.

I stand in front of my students
telling them about sentence fragments.
I ask them to find the ten fragments
in the twenty-one-sentence paragraph on page forty-five.
They've come from all parts
of the world — Iran, Micronesia, Africa,
Japan, China, even Los Angeles — and they're still
eager to please me. It's less than half
way through the quarter.

They bend over their books and begin.
Hamid's lips move as he follows
the tortuous labyrinth of English syntax.
Yoshie sits erect, perfect in her pale make-up,
legs crossed, quick pulse minutely
jerking her right foot. Tony
sprawls limp in his desk, relaxed
as only someone can be who's
from an island in the South Pacific.

The melody floats around and through us
in the room, broken here and there, fragmented,
re-started. It feels mideastern, but
it could be jazz, or the blues — it could be
anything from anywhere.
I sit down on my desk to wait,
and it hits me from nowhere — a sudden
sweet, almost painful love for my students.

"Nevermind," I want to cry out.
"It doesn't matter about fragments.
Finding them or not. Everything's
a fragment and everything's not a fragment.
Listen to the music, how fragmented,
how whole, how we can't separate the music
from the sun falling on its knees on all the greenness,
from this moment, how this moment
contains all the fragments of yesterday
and everything we'll ever know of tomorrow!"

Instead, I keep a coward's silence.
The music stops abruptly;
they finish their work,
and we go through the right answers,
which is to say
we separate the fragments from the whole.

BIOGRAPHIES

KIM ADDONIZIO writes: "Like all writers, I write out of my obsessions. I try to turn over the rocks and watch carefully what teems underneath them, what crawls out, what scuttles away. I'm interested in the darkness and disorder, and in how we can manage to live with grace in an increasingly graceless world. Lately I find myself writing more and more about "marginal" characters: the old, the dispossessed, the damaged, the failed dreamers who go on dreaming. I've worked as a waitress, cook, secretary, portrait photographer, tennis instructor, and attendant for the disabled, did a five-year stint in an auto parts store, and am now teaching writing and studying rhetoric. I have work in *Three West Coast Women* (Five Fingers Poetry) and a few journals, and I'm completing a new manuscript, *The Philosopher's Club*."

ALTA is the founder of Shameless Hussy Press which became, in 1969, America's first feminist publishing house. Her latest book, *Deluged with Dudes: Memoirs of a Shameless Hussy*, was published by AP Northcott. Having raised two children, she is currently battling the empty nest blues at her home in Berkeley. She collects quilts and BMWs.

ANTLER spends several months alone in the wilderness each year. He earns his living at part-time jobs like housepainting to enjoy maximum freedom to work on his poetry. He has performed his work extensively on East and West coasts as well as in "Inland Ocean Realms," and tries to live up to Whitman's invocation of the poet as "itinerant gladness scatterer." In 1980 City Lights published *Factory* and in 1986 Ballantine published *Last Words*, a fuller collection of his work.

FRANK BIDART grew up in Bakersfield, California, studied at U.C. Riverside, and then did graduate work at Harvard where he was a student of Robert Lowell's, a relationship that developed into an intimate friendship, one which Bidart has characterized as "a profound event in my life: a *healing* event." In an interview with Mark Halliday, Bidart says: "So much of our ordinary lives seems to refuse us — seems almost dedicated to denying us — knowledge of what is beneath the relatively unexceptionable surface of repeated social and economic relations. The artist's problem is to make life *show* itself. . . . Again and again, insight is dramatized by showing the conflict between what is ordinarily seen, ordinarily understood, and what now is experienced as real. Cracking the shell of the world; or finding that the shell is cracking under you. The unrealizable ideal is to write as if the earth opened and spoke." His collections of poetry include *Golden State, The Book of the Body,* and *The Sacrifice.*

LAUREL ANN BOGEN has served as Executive Director of the Los Angeles Poetry Theater, was a poetry performance instructor at the Beyond Baroque Foundation and is a frequent performer of her own work in and around Los Angeles. "Poetry," she says, "has saved my life— or at least given it meaning." Her most recent books are *Do Iguanas Dance, Under the Moonlight; The Projects;* and *Rag Tag We Kiss,* all from Illuminati Press.

LOVERNE BROWN writes: "My early childhood was spent in Southwestern Alaska; after time in Upper Michigan and Berkeley I returned to the Territory to be a news reporter on a daily paper in Juneau. Still later, my husband and I edited our own paper in Seldovia. For the past more than 30 years I have lived in San Diego. I feel the only reason for writing poetry is to convey to someone else the emotion which evoked it and I never feel a poem is complete until someone other than myself has read it. Would I then write if I were marooned on the proverbial desert island? Yes — because I am a complete optimist and would want to be ready when a man- or woman-Friday turned up as my first truly captive audience." Her books include *The View from the End of the Pier* (Gorilla Press) and *Gathering Wine Grapes at the Hollywood Hilton* (La Querencia Press: Box 3120, Hillcrest Station, San Diego, CA 92103).

CHARLES BUKOWSKI began writing poetry at the age of 35 after coming out of the death ward at L.A. County General Hospital. In a recent interview with *The New York Quarterly* he commented: "I have compassion for almost all the individuals of the world; at the same time, they repulse me. . . . Actually I am not a tough person and sexually, most of the time, I am almost a prude, but I am often a nasty drunk and many strange things happen to me when I'm drunk. . . . For me to get paid for writing is like going to bed with a beautiful woman and afterwards she gets up, goes to her purse and gives me a handful of money. I'll take it." Most of his collections of poetry and fiction are published by Black Sparrow Press. The movie *Barfly* was written by Bukowski while the films *Tales of Ordinary Madness* and *Love Is a Dog From Hell* are based on his stories.

RAYMOND CARVER has had two superb collections of poetry published in the past few years: *Where Water Comes Together With Other Water* and *Ultramarine.* Published by Random House in 1985 and '86, they are now out in Vintage Paperbacks. In 1988 Atlantic Monthly Press published *Where I'm Calling From: New and Selected Stories.* Carver, one of America's most celebrated writers, died in the summer of 1988.

MARION COHEN writes: "I'm committed to keeping my poetry sensitive, kind, authentic, and childlike when called for. I don't like unhappy endings, but I'm great on unhappy middles." Among several recent volumes she has published *An Ambitious Sort of Grief: Diary of Neo-Natal Loss; A Garden Flower: Diary of Life After Cesarean Birth;* and *The Sitting-Down Hug: Poems on Living with a Disabled Partner.* All three are from The Liberal Press (Box 160361, Las Colinas, TX 75016).

WANDA COLEMAN writes: "I go home a lot — as often as possible. I've never moved far from it. I see/cherish my parents often and walk familiar Watts streets through the eyes of an angry adolescence. These days I feel the stress/battle fatigue; my war is an ongoing wage of words/wills writing has become for me/self declared. Like classic tales of the Old Warrior, who longs/I long for a peace — irony being there will be no peace in my lifetime. (I define peace as being free of the constraints of racism.) So I force myself to sit at the typewriter and strike blows." Her recent books are *Mad Dog Black Lady, Imagoes* and *Heavy Daughter Blues*, all from Black Sparrow Press.

BILLY COLLINS writes: "I write poetry not because there is something special I have to say, some message on a ribboned scroll, but because the act of composition is a game that I almost always find interesting. For me the most vital part of a line of poetry, alone on a page, is its capacity to suggest another line. In this way, one thing is always leading to another, each line begetting the next line like all those teeming beings in Genesis. At some point, the poem starts running down, and the lines become less fecund, less willing to produce other lines. Finally, a line is written that refuses to give forth another one; then I hit the period key. Some of the results of this hatching will appear this year in a collection called *The Apple That Astonished Paris* (University of Arkansas Press)."

GREGORY CORSO, a visionary poet and a central literary figure of the Beat Generation, grew up in foster homes and on the streets of New York City. Of his youthful and transformative prison stint, Corso has written, "Sometimes hell is a good place — if it proves to one that because it exists, so must its opposite, heaven, exist. And what was that heaven? Poetry." He has written that the poet "stands merely as a man, a man who feels that he is but the guardian of the human consciousness and that when he dies there will be another poet to take his relay, in order that consciousness grow ever more perfect, and man ever more human, and life ever more total." *Herald of the Autochthonic Spirit* was published by New Directions in 1981.

JAYNE CORTEZ, who has performed her poetry alone and with music throughout the United States, Africa, Europe and Latin America, is the author of six collections of poetry, the most recent of which is *Coagulations: New & Selected Poems,* from Thunder's Mouth Press. *Maintain Control* is the latest of four recordings of her work. She lives in New York City.

DIANE DI PRIMA was a central figure in the New York contingent of the Beat/ Black Mountain poetry revolution of the 1960's. With LeRoi Jones she co-edited *The Floating Bear,* an influential newsletter, between 1962 and '64 and was sole editor until 1970. She helped found the New York Poets' Theatre in 1961 and established Poets Press in 1964. In 1968 she moved to the Bay Area. A playwright and fiction writer as well as a poet, the hip-bohemian consciousness of her early writing has been fused to a passionate political and feminist commitment. She has been a faculty member of the Naropa Institute and of the New College of California, and is a member of the Zen Center of San Francisco. Her *Selected Poems: 1956-1976* is published by North Atlantic Books.

STEPHEN DOBYNS teaches in the creative writing program at Syracuse University and in the MFA program at Warren Wilson College. His sixth book of poems, *Cemetery Nights,* was published by Viking in 1987. His ninth novel, *The Two Deaths of Senora Puccini,* will be published by Viking in the summer of 1988. Four of his other novels are a series of mysteries set in Saratoga Springs, New York. The fifth in that series, *Saratoga Bestiary,* will be published by Viking in January, 1989.

LAURIE DUESING writes: "Although both my parents are artists, I did not begin writing seriously until I was thirty-seven years old and was admitted to Alan Soldofsky's Poems in Progress class offered at UC extension. I was tired of lurching from relationship to relationship and decided I'd better work on something that would never leave me. It has worked so well I have decided I will never leave it. John Logan, one of my first teachers under the auspices of Alan's class, described me as the one who wrote "the narrative body poems." I think that is about right. I like the physical world and any way I can participate in it. I am a member of a women's whaleboat rowing team (strictly grunt work), and though I am too tall and too old, I am also a serious student of ballet. I have taught composition and creative writing at Solano Community College for the last twenty years. At the risk of sounding like a mush mouth, I admit I love my work." A selection of her poems appears in *Three West Coast Women*, published by Five Fingers Press.

LAWRENCE FERLINGHETTI is a poet, novelist, painter, translator, playwright, bookstore proprietor and publisher of one of America's most important poetry presses, City Lights Books. He is a passionate, socially committed populist writer who was a member of the literary demolition squad that broke through the ponderous conventions of formalist verse and helped revivify American poetry in the 1950s and '60s. In 1981, New Directions published Ferlinghetti's *Endless Life: Selected Poems*.

EDWARD FIELD writes: "I discovered poetry when I was in the air force in WWII. Then, in 1948 on a ship to France after giving up on NYU, I was lucky enough to meet Robert Friend, poet and teacher, and somehow he unlocked my tongue. As years of rejections piled up . . . I was also trying to become more real, in poetry and life. So it is hard to understand how, for so many poets, poetry is also an exercise in snobbery, for whom poetry means being superior, to prefer their poems cool, elegant, artificial, cryptic. I automatically identify with what snobs look down on— the slobs, the underdog, for whom poetry is an act of rebellion, the secret voice speaking out, however crudely, as in my first book's title *Stand Up, Friend, With Me.* These days I live in NYC, spend as much time in Europe as possible, and besides poetry, write novels." His most recent book is *New and Selected Poems: From the Book of My Life* (Sheep Meadow Press).

ALLEN GINSBERG has been a seminal figure in world poetry and American culture since the publication of *Howl* in 1956. Revivifying the visionary poetic tradition of Blake and Whitman, he was largely responsible for shattering conventional constraints and giving our poetry a new emotional, spiritual and linguistic openness. After beginning meditation practice under Chogyam Trungpa, Rinpoche, in 1972, Ginsberg extended his poetic practice to public improvisation on blues chords with political Dharma themes. Harper & Row has published his three latest books: *Collected Poems 1947-1980, White Shroud: Poems 1980-1985,* and *Howl, Annotated with original manuscripts.*

JUDY GRAHN writes: "Maverick just happens to be the kind of car I drive; I bought my first and, so far, only car when I was 42. The poems in this collection exemplify my desire to express ordinary lives as the extraordinary events they are, and yet find a group identity as a place to live. Can there be groups of mavericks? Sometimes I understand myself as one of the cows, nurturing, driven, in the center of the herd; sometimes I must tangle horns with the wild countryside. I both thrilled and shocked myself, and others, by calling my first book *Edward the Dyke and Other Poems.* Since 1980 I have been deeply exploring women's mythology in my poetry, *The Queen of Wands*, The Crossing Press, 1982; and *The Queen of Swords*, Beacon Press, 1987. I have also written nonfiction, especially *Another Mother Tongue*, Beacon Press, 1984, a Gay and Lesbian cultural history. My current ambition is to set Gertrude Stein's poetry to synthesizer music."

JACK GRAPES is a poet, playwright, teacher and professional actor (*Hill Street Blues, MASH,* etc.). He recently played the lead role in *Circle of Will*, a bizarre, metaphysical comedy about Shakespeare, which he co-authored with Bill Cakmis. The play had a successful run in L.A. and Grapes is currently writing the lyrics for a musical version. He teaches in the California Poets in the Schools program and at UCLA Extension. The author of a number of collections of poetry, his most recent is *Trees, Coffee, and the Eyes of Deer* from Bombshelter Press, 6421½ Orange Street, L.A., CA 90048.

JANA HARRIS was born in San Francisco and grew up near Clackamas, Oregon— a defunct mill town. She recalls that at the University of Oregon, "When my Contemporary Literature professor asked: What is the symbolism of Hemingway's protagonist standing at a second story window watching her husband down in the street . . . wearing a raincoat (the answer had something to do with the kind of prophylactic her husband was using and thereby preventing her from fulfilling herself as a woman), I knew I was never going to make it in English Literature." She taught algebra for 6 years and in the Bay Area "became a part of that wonderful 'poetry for the public' reading scene which flourished and nurtured young writers during the early seventies." She helped found *Poetry Flash*, then moved to New York & Princeton before returning to the Northwest where she lives on a farm raising horses among neighbors who "make use of their freedom of religion and their right to bear arms, giving the first and second amendments a complete work-out every day." She is the author of a novel and five collections of poetry. The Smith recently republished her collection *The Clackamas.*

DAVID KIRBY was born in Louisiana but has lived in France and Italy and now resides in Tallahassee, where he teaches English at Florida State University. His books include *Sarah Bernhardt's Leg, Saving the Young Men of Vienna,* and *Diving For Poems: Where Poetry Comes From and How to Write It* (the latter from Word Beat Press). He is currently writing a book on Mark Strand who "is as different from me as any writer I know, so maybe I can learn something from him."

RON KOERTGE, author of *The Boogeyman*, a novel published by Norton, has recently taken to writing novels for young adults. *Where the Kissing Never Stops* came out in **1986** and *The Arizona Kid* in **1988**. The author of a number of brilliant collections of poetry, his selected poems, *Life on the Edge of the Continent*, is published by the University of Arkansas Press. He writes, "A lot of my poems are about living in the middle of the country, about being brought up as a Baptist and then carrying all that with me through Arizona (graduate school) and then into California where I teach and live . . . . I will go anywhere in any weather to bet on a horserace."

STEVE KOWIT is involved in the Animal Rights movement to stop the torture and extermination of our fellow beings in laboratories, slaughterhouses and in the wild. He is also one of a growing number of American Jews agitating for the rights of the Palestinian people. Many of his poems are slapstick tales that turn on the ego's genius for self-deception. His inner work has involved Gurdjieffian and Buddhist studies. His books include *Passionate Journey* and *Lurid Confessions*.

JOANNE KYGER was born in Vallejo, California, studied at U.C. Santa Barbara, then moved to the Bay Area and became part of the Duncan-Spicer circle of the late 50's. After starting Zen practice with Shunryu Suzuki she moved to Japan where she lived from 1960 to 1964, during which time she also traveled extensively in India. One of the central figures of the Beat Generation's renewal of American poetry, she has made her home in Bolinas, California, since 1969. Her books include *All This Every Day* (Big Sky Books), *The Wonderful Focus of You* (Z Press), *Up My Coast* (Floating Island Books), and *Mexico Blondé* (Evergreen Press).

DORIANNE LAUX lives in Berkeley with her 11-year-old daughter, Tristem, and attends Mills College in Oakland. She writes: "To attempt to write poetry is to try to capture on paper, in words, that which is unfathomable, ineffable, irreducible, and therefore, inexpressible." She has worked for the Domestic Violence Prevention Project in the Oakland public schools and has poetry and commentary forthcoming in *Healing Ourselves: A Guide for Survivors of Child Sexual Abuse*, where she speaks as a poet, facilitator and survivor. An extended selection of her poetry can be found in *Three West Coast Women*, published in 1987 by Five Fingers Poetry.

NAOMI LAZARD writes: "I started out by studying design. My course changed when I took a poetry workshop with John Logan. I had always been a voracious reader but never thought of writing until then. My passions have never altered: justice, animals, language." Two of her recently published books are *Ordinances* (Owl Creek Press), and *The True Subject: Selected Poems of Faiz Hamad Faiz* (Princeton University Press), a project she and the great Pakistani poet worked on from 1979 until his death in 1984. Most recently she has co-authored a screenplay dealing with the confrontation between Native American culture and Christianity.

GERALD LOCKLIN claims that if we printed the truth about his life, nobody would read him. "It's bad enough," he says, "that my personality or lack of it sometimes sneaks into my poems." Locklin, who teaches at California State University Long Beach, has been an influential figure in the Long Beach/L.A. poetry scene for many years. The author of numerous collections of poetry and fiction, three of which have been published in German translations, he has published most recently *The Case of the Missing Blue Volkswagen* with Applezaba Press, *A Constituency of Dunces* with Slipstream Press, *Children of a Lesser Demagogue* with Wormwood Review Press, *On The Rack* with Trout Creek Press, and *The Death of Jean-Paul Sartre* with Ghost Pony Press.

PHILLIP LOPATE has published two novels, two books of nonfiction and two collections of poetry. He writes: "I like direct statement and irony in poetry; I shy away from metaphor and traditional image-making. Some poets who have influenced me include Cavafy, Pavese, Frank O'Hara, Randall Jarrell (late), Reznikoff, Neruda, Vallejo, Pasternak, Williams. . . . For all its recent disparagement, I see nothing terribly wrong with humanism and wouldn't mind being categorized as a psychological humanist (urban variety)." His collections of poetry are *The Eyes Don't Always Want To Stay Open* and *The Daily Round*, both from Sun Press. His latest book was *The Rug Merchant*, a novel published by Viking in 1987 and reprinted as a Penguin paperback in '88.

HANK MALONE spent several years as an ABC radio talk-show host and as a print journalist. He presently works in private practice as a psychotherapist in the Detroit area. His most recent collections are *The Fashion Model and the Astronaut* from Detroit River Press; *Survival, Evasion, and Escape* from La Jolla Poets Press; and *Wet Finger Held to the Breeze* from Pearl Magazine. His books can be ordered directly from him at 23564 Rensselaer, Oak Park, MI 48203.

JOSÉ MONTOYA writes: "I began my life's journey at the tail-end of the great depression in long relief lines and the W.P.A. During the upheavals of World War II, I got to experience the barrios of Albuquerque and the bleak, albeit exciting, adventure of trekking West on Route 66 to California to pick fruit and live in labor camps until my father, just a few years out of Leavenworth for bootlegging and contraband — had to survive the depression, *que no?* — decided the shipyards paid better wages than the fields. So Oakland and Alameda and discovering Jack London. . . . Korea guaranteed me the G.I. Bill and I studied to become an artist but that austere future loomed unacceptable so I became an art teacher. . . . I train young prospective teachers at CSU Sacramento to use the healing magic of art with children to safeguard and insure the future of mankind. I enjoy what I do and it leaves me time to paint and write about the plight of the Chicano People. And I also sing and write about it with the Trio Casindio and the Royal Chicano Air Force. *Chicano Music All Day* is the name of our album."

HAROLD NORSE writes: "In Brooklyn at age 17, having read *Leaves of Grass*, *Flowers of Evil* and *The Bridge*, I experienced a sort of cosmic oneness with Whitman, Baudelaire and Crane, vowing that I'd spend my life scribbling poetry and prose about the love of comrades, about being a rose-lipped maiden *and* a lightfoot lad (at the same time) and even about out-of-the-body astral voyages (Baudelaire's "anywhere out of this world!"). The campus of Brooklyn College then (my alma mater) was near Columbia Heights where Crane had lived and written *The Bridge*, and where Whitman first set up *Leaves of Grass* on Cranberry Street. Many years and 14 books later not much has changed for me except for some gross cynical changes, but my scribblings have attracted, if not a wide international following, a smallish but loyal one, in several languages. A N.Y. *Times* book reviewer, writing in the S.F. *Chronicle* about my latest volume, *The Love Poems* (Crossing Press) said: 'Eros . . . drives these poems forward until the repetition of the sexual imagery breaks out of the sexual realm altogether and becomes a heroic movement toward personal, non-sexual human contact and relatedness.' This puts it neatly; I cannot add to it."

SHARON OLDS writes: "I'm a woman living in New York City, beside the Hudson River. I'm Western; born in San Francisco, I spent summers in the Sierra Nevada mountains. I was born in the middle of World War II, grew up near a school for the blind, and attended an Episcopalian church made of redwood. In Jr. High and High School I read and read poetry, memorized it, was in love with it. After I was 30 I stopped trying to make my poems sound like other people's. Also, I saw the generation before mine doing what I wanted to do: write about family, about children, in lines that gave each poem its own shape, its own body. Gradually, the idea of *family* expanded to include New York City, Guatemala, anywhere. I teach at Goldwater Hospital, on Roosevelt Island (a 900-bed public hospital for the physically disabled), and at N.Y.U. I love baseball. I love Koko the gorilla and hope she will have a child." Sharon Olds' books include *Satan Says, The Dead and the Living,* and *The Gold Cell.*

SIMON ORTIZ writes: "I find it hard to write these days actually. Years ago, it was easier; it seemed I didn't really have to think, or even feel much, at least not deliberately. Just *feel* and let it flow, something like that. Now, it's a matter of enough time to write. Not much of it. So the time I do have is precious, and I believe the struggle to write makes me more aware in a concrete sense of the power of words. It makes me more aware of the sharing of this power with all things: this is the struggle perhaps, to know that using language is in concert with all life. I'm writing fewer poems and stories than I ever have, but for some reason I feel more than ever that I'm doing what I'm supposed to be doing as a writer/lover of language." A collection of Simon Ortiz's poetry, *A Good Journey,* is available from the University of Arizona Press.

DAN PROPPER grew up in Williamsburg, Brooklyn. He remembers when he was 12 "radios going in open windows, and every once in a while something alive came through, like 'Caldonia,' 'Hey Ba Ba Re Bop,' 'Open the Door Richard,' 'Orange-Colored Sky.' 2 years later I was a paper-boy folding my newspapers after school listening to black music from Newark and Harlem, deejays Jack 'Pearshape' Walker and Georgie Hudson, I was the Johnnie Otis of Bayside Queens, my friends thought I was crazy. . . . I wanted to grow up and be a hipster, a musician, play tenor sax in Basie's band. . . . For my 20th birthday I treated myself to an evening in a new place, The Five Spot. Heard Monk and Coltrane. Stopped what I was doing and went every night after work at Decca and classes at the New School. Became a waiter at the Five Spot. Discovered poetry (Juan Ramon Jimenez, then Allen Ginsberg). Earliest poem worth keeping 3/58." Dan Propper's *Tale of the Amazing Tramp* was published by Cherry Valley Editions, and *For Kerouac in Heaven* was published by Energy Press. *Fable of the Final Hour* is being republished by Water Row Books (Box 438, Sudbury, MA).

KAREN SNOW is the pseudonym for a reclusive writer. After attending the University of Michigan, she married a fellow student, lived a while in London, and raised two sons. When the sons had gone off to college, Ms. Snow resumed writing, and her novel *Willo* was published in 1976 by Street Fiction Press, then re-issued in paperback by Pinnacle Books. In 1978 her book of poems, *Wonders,* was published by Viking. Three years later, Countryman Press published *Outsiders,* a book of poetry and prose. Her collection of sixteen short stories is currently in submission, as well as her new and selected poems. She and her husband recently moved to Arizona.

GARY SNYDER was raised in rural Washington state not far from Puget Sound. He worked in logging camps, with the National Forest Service and as a merchant marine, did graduate work in linguistics and Oriental languages, and then in 1956 traveled to Japan to pursue studies in Far Eastern culture, Zen Buddhist texts and Renzai Zen practice. He returned to reside again in the United States in 1969. Since 1970 he has been living on a farmstead in the northern Sierra Nevada, making frequent trips to Alaska and Hawaii with occasional travels to Japan, Europe, Australia and China. Snyder is the founder of the Ring of Bone Zendo, a member of the Advisory Board of the Friends of the Earth and one of the hemisphere's leading spokespeople for ecological sanity and the preservation of wilderness. He is also one of our leading poets. His recent books include *Axe Handles* and *Left Out in the Rain: New Poems 1947-1985*.

AUSTIN STRAUS is an artist and political activist as well as a poet. A former regional coordinator for Amnesty International, he presently teaches at UCLA, LA City College and in Southern California prisons. His work in the visual arts includes collages, sun-etchings (burnt paper works), zinc-plate etchings, and one-of-a-kind books. A cartoon series, "Poetickles," appears monthly in LA's poetry newsletter, *Shattersheet*. He is married to the poet Wanda Coleman with whom he co-hosts the KPFK-FM program "The Poetry Connexion."

AL ZOLYNAS was born in 1945 in Austria of Lithuanian parents displaced by the war. He spent his early childhood in Germany and in Australian migrant camps. Since then he has moved over a score of times through Sydney, Chicago, Utah, Minnesota, and California—this nomadic life contributing to a sense of rootlessness. The search for "home" has been through writing and the practice of Zen. He has been a Hunger Project volunteer and teaches at U.S. International University, San Diego. His poems attempt to recreate and honor the essential mystery of being. His collection, *The New Physics*, is available from Wesleyan University Press.

ACKNOWLEDGEMENTS

Grateful acknowledgement is made to the following for permission to reprint material copyrighted by them:

KIM ADDONIZIO: "The Call" and "Break" are reprinted from *Three West Coast Women*. Copyright ©1987 by Kim Addonizio. By permission of Five Fingers Press.

ALTA: "all those men puppy dogging," "LOL," "the old wicker chair unravelling," "the girls with their young breasts," "ah. yr. angry," and "joy comes so softly" are reprinted from *No Visible Means of Support*. Copyright ©1971 by Alta. By permission of the author. "That chick is SO REVOLUTIONARY" is reprinted from *I Am Not a Practicing Angel*. Copyright ©1976 by Alta. By permission of The Crossing Press.

ANTLER: "Your Poetry's No Good Because It Tries to Convey a Message," "Childfoot Visitation," "Rexroth As He Appeared To Exist, May 24, 1968 9:00 PM," and excerpt from part x of "Factory" are reprinted from *Last Words*. Copyright ©1986 by Antler. By permission of Available Press, Ballantine Books, a division of Random House, Inc.

FRANK BIDART: "Another Life" is reprinted from *Golden State*. Copyright ©1973 by Frank Bidart. By permission of George Braziller, Inc. Publishers.

LAUREL ANN BOGEN: "I Coulda Been a Contender" and "I Eat Lunch With a Schizophrenic" are reprinted from *Do Iguanas Dance, Under the Moonlight*. Copyright ©1984 by Laurel Ann Bogen. By permission of Illuminati Press.

LOVERNE BROWN: "A Sunday Morning After a Saturday Night," "Wild Geese," "The Warning," "A Very Wet Leavetaking," and "A Meeting of Mavericks" are reprinted from *View from the End of the Pier*. Copyright ©1983 by LoVerne Brown. By permission of Gorilla Press. "Checkmate" is reprinted from *Gathering Wine Grapes at the Hollywood Hilton*. Copyright ©1986 by LoVerne Brown. Printed by permission of La Querencia Press.

CHARLES BUKOWSKI: "Beans With Garlic" is reprinted from *Burning in Water, Drowning in Flames: Selected Poems 1955-1973*. Copyright ©1965 by Charles Bukowski. "Clean Old Man" and "The Insane Always Loved Me" are reprinted from *Love Is a Dog From Hell*. "The Proud Thin Dying" and "The Drill" are reprinted from *Play the Piano Drunk Like a Percussion Instrument Until the Fingers Begin to Bleed a Bit*. Copyright ©1979 by Charles Bukowski. "History of a Tough Motherfucker" and "Take It" are reprinted from *War All the Time*. Copyright ©1984 by Charles Bukowski. By permission of Black Sparrow Press.

RAYMOND CARVER: "Blood," "The Hat," "Rain," "The Party" and "Interview" are reprinted from *Where Water Comes Together With Other Water* (published by Random House). Copyright ©1985 by Ramond Carver. "Cobweb" and "The Author of Her Misfortune" are reprinted from *Ultramarine* (published by Random House). Copyright ©1986 by Raymond Carver. By permission of the author.

MARION COHEN: "Teaching Sturm-Louville" and "Children Grow At Night" are reprinted from *The Weirdest is the Sphere: The Math Poems* (published by 7 Woods Press). Copyright ©1979 by Marion Cohen. By permission of the author.

WANDA COLEMAN: "Somewhere," "Luz" and "Untitled" are reprinted from *Mad Dog Black Lady*. Copyright ©1979 by Wanda Coleman. By permission of Black Sparrow Press.

BILLY COLLINS: "Flames" and "Embrace" are reprinted from *The Apple That Astonished Paris*. Copyright ©1987 by Billy Collins. By permission of The University of Arkansas Press. "The Willies" copyright ©1988 by Billy Collins. By permission of the author.

GREGORY CORSO: "Italian Extravaganza," "In a Dull Furnished Room" and "The Mad Yak" are reprinted from *Gasoline*. Copyright ©1958 by Gregory Corso. By permission of City Light Books. "The Whole Mess . . . Almost" is reprinted from *Herald of the Autochthonic Spirit*. Copyright ©1981 by Gregory Corso. By permission of New Directions Publishing Corporation.

JAYNE CORTEZ: "Rape," "I See Chano Pozo" and "They Came Again in 1970 in 1980" are reprinted from *Coagulations*. Copyright ©1987 by Jayne Cortez (Thunder's Mouth Press). By permission of the author.

DIANE DI PRIMA: "Letter to Jeanne (at Tassajara)," "Biology Lesson," "For Roi" and "The Journey" are reprinted from *Selected Poems 1956-1976* (published by North Atlantic Books). Copyright ©1977 by Diane di Prima. By permission of the author.

STEPHEN DOBYNS: "Creeping Intelligence" and "White Pig" are reprinted from *Cemetery Nights*. Copyright ©1987 by Stephen Dobyns. By permission of Viking Penguin, Inc.

LAURIE DUESING: "The Valley Lounge" and "A Miracle" are reprinted from *Three West Coast Women*. Copyright ©1987 by Laurie Duesing. By permission of Five Fingers Press.

EDWARD FIELD: "The Farewell" is reprinted from *A Full Heart* (published by Sheep Meadow Press). Copyright ©1977 by Edward Field. "Donkeys" and "A Journey" are reprinted from *New and Selected Poems* (published by Sheep Meadow Press). Copyright ©1987 by Edward Field. "World War II" is reprinted from *Variety Photoplays* (published by Maelstrom Press). Copyright ©1977 by Edward Field. By permission of the author.

LAWRENCE FERLINGHETTI: "The Love Nut" is reprinted from *Landscapes of Living & Dying*. Copyright ©1979 by Lawrence Ferlinghetti. "Two Scavengers in a Truck, Two Beautiful People in a Mercedes" is reprinted from *Endless Life: Selected Poems*. Copyright ©1978 by Lawrence Ferlinghetti. By permission of New Directions.

ALLEN GINSBERG: "Dream Record: June 8, 1955," copyright ©1955 by Allen Ginsberg. "Death to Van Gogh's Ear!" copyright ©1958 by Allen Ginsberg. "To Lindsay," copyright ©1958 by Allen Ginsberg. "To Lindsay," copyright ©1958 by Allen Ginsberg. "Rain-Wet Asphalt Heat, Garbage Curbed Cans Overflowing," copyright ©1969 by Allen Ginsberg. "Over Denver Again," copyright ©1969 by Allen Ginsberg. "What Would You Do If You Lost It," copyright ©1973 by Allen Ginsberg. "Spring Fashions," copyright ©1979 by Allen Ginsberg. Reprinted from *Collected Poems 1947-1980*. By permission of Harper & Row Publishers, Inc.

JUDY GRAHN: "Ella, in a Square Apron, Along Highway 80," "Vera, from My Childhood," "A Woman Is Talking to Death: Part Three," "I have only one reason for living," "Love rode 1500 miles on a grey. . . ." and "Ah, Love you smell of petroleum" are reprinted from *The Work of A Common Woman: Collected Poetry (1964-1977)*. Copyright ©1987 by Judy Grahn. By permission of The Crossing Press.